Santo Domingo and After

The Challenges for the Latin American Church

Gustavo Gutiérrez

Francis McDonagh

Cândido Padin OSB

Jon Sobrino SJ

First published 1993

Catholic Institute for International Relations (CIIR)
Unit 3 Canonbury Yard, 190a New North Road,
London N1 7BJ, UK

British Library Cataloguing-in-
Publication Data
A catalogue record for this book
is available from the British Library.

ISBN 1 85287 120 2

Printed in England by the Russell Press Ltd.

Cover and text design by Jan Brown Designs

Contents

Introduction

The October 1992 Latin American bishops' conference in Santo Domingo is the latest milestone in a 30-year journey of the Latin American church. Since the 1960s the Roman Catholic Church in Latin America has been news. At times newspaper readers might have been forgiven for thinking that the bishops of Latin America had abjured the centuries-old alliance of cross and sword and joined the revolution. Both poles of that contrast are mythology, but the headlines did reflect a change in the Latin American church that was little short of revolutionary.

The key event at the beginning of this process was the General Conference of Latin American bishops at Medellín, Colombia, in 1968, where the bishops committed the church to work for justice and to changing social, economic and political structures as well as seeking to change hearts.

Medellín was part of a process which moved significant sections of the Latin American church from the side of the rulers to the side of the masses. In many cases this meant a physical move, as when Cardinal Arns in São Paulo sold his palace to build community centres in poor districts, or when priests and sisters abandoned rich parishes and elite schools to promote base communities in the slums and shantytowns. This process became known as 'the preferential option for the poor', ratified at the Third General Conference of Latin American Bishops, at Puebla, Mexico, in 1979, and 'liberation theology', its intellectual elaboration, became one of the main strands in theology in the world church.

1

This process had clear political implications, noted by the famous Rockefeller Report of 1969, though less in dramatic shifts of allegiance, as in the case of priests who joined the guerrillas, such as Camilo Torres in Colombia, or Fr Gaspar García Laviana in Nicaragua, than in a gradual growth among ordinary people in a sense of their own dignity and rights. Such people were less likely to accept without question the leadership of traditional elites, and readier to support the Sandinistas in Nicaragua, the Farabundo Martí National Liberation Front (FMLN) in El Salvador, or the Workers' Party (PT) in Brazil.

The transformation, however, produced fierce opposition within the Latin American church, and a rearguard action was soon mounted by an alliance of conservative prelates in Latin America and the Vatican. The 1979 Puebla conference was the scene of fierce debate over the direction of the Latin American church, and the conservative pressure was even stronger around the Santo Domingo conference.

The Santo Domingo bishops' conference is analysed in this book from various points of view. First there is an account by a CIIR observer, a European, drawing on CIIR's many years of friendship with a wide range of figures in the church in Latin America, but remaining, in the end, an outsider's view. The other voices are those of insiders, and the variety of tones in these voices is also significant.

Fr Jon Sobrino expresses the hurt and anger widely felt in Latin America at the manipulation of the Santo Domingo conference. It is a manipulation which not only caused pain and insult to many who have borne the burden of the day and the heat in Latin America, but which also threatens the church's ability to be a credible messenger of liberation, communion and participation.

Fr Gustavo Gutiérrez, the 'father of liberation theology', stresses what there is in common, from Vatican II, through Medellín and Puebla to Santo Domingo, for the majority of bishops of Latin America. He notes that, in the teaching of the often criticised John Paul II, the preferential option for the poor has entered the universal ordinary magisterium of the Catholic Church.

Bishop Cândido Padin was one of the victims of Santo Domingo. His letter, in fact a short essay in canon law, is important as a record of the relationship between the Vatican and a particular church. This is a crucial issue for Catholics throughout the world, and is being raised in a particular way in 1993 in the synod for Africa, which is a synod, that is to say, has less autonomy than a conference of bishops, and is taking place, not in Africa, but in Rome. But respect — or the lack of it — for freedom of expression and personal dignity within the Roman Catholic Church is also closely observed by its partners in ecumenical dialogue.

Above all, however, the way the church acts, and where it places itself in society, has profound human implications, social, economic and political, in a sense much more important than the sterile debate about whether the 'option for the poor' is Marxist. The presence of bishops, priests and religious, men but even more women, with poor communities throughout Latin America may not always have brought much improvement in their material conditions, but has helped them to stay human and to survive. This is the role of base communities today in impoverished post-Sandinista Nicaragua, and in many parts of an increasingly unequal continent.

Perhaps the most serious challenge the world faces today is to create an economic and social order which employs and benefits from the skills of all the world's population and does not devastate natural resources. The trend to integration in the world economy based on the high-technology economies of the United States, the European Community and Japan is leaving much of the world's population surplus to economic requirements. This trend is also evident within regional and national economies, as evidenced by the difference between western, eastern and southern Europe, or the 'underclass' produced in the United States and Britain since 1979.

What might be labelled the liberal approach to this challenge is structural adjustment, measures to help the surplus people come to terms with their lot. The approach of those in the Latin American church who have made an option for the poor, the defenders of Indian rights, the champions of land reform, of the unemployed, all those who struggle to survive, is quite different. It is based on the radical utopia of Jesus, the image of the meal in which all are fed and there is food to spare or, in a different Christian language, the belief that every human being is of inestimable worth. This approach is now trying to absorb the indigenous attitude of respect for the earth as our mother. The 'church of the poor' in Latin America has tried to bring this utopia about by empowering the marginalised. It is this empowerment which seems to arouse concern in the Vatican, but the premises of this concern need closer examination. Hostility to the empowerment of the poor often seemed to be based on the belief in a 'third way', between capitalism and communism. The collapse of 'real socialism' has made this schema redundant and, in practice, in Latin America opposition to the 'preferential option for the poor' is equivalent to support for a social and political model which excludes the majority of Latin Americans from full citizenship and relies on hunger or repression to sustain it. Rejection of the poor as full human beings is the logical implication, perhaps not always conscious, of the model of church the Roman curia brought to Santo Domingo.

CIIR
September 1993

The Santo Domingo Conference

FRANCIS McDONAGH

I. THE TRADITION OF VATICAN II

The transformation of the Latin American church in the last 30 years is sometimes treated as an example of spontaneous combustion, a development peculiar to Latin America. In fact, however, the transformation is in the main line of developments in the universal church. The Medellín conference of 1968 was a direct response to the Second Vatican Council (1962-65), summoned by Pope John XXIII to 'open the windows' of the church to the experience and aspirations of all people of good will. At the heart of the Council was the recognition that the mission of the church is in the world, sharing 'the joys and hopes, griefs and anxieties of the people of this age' (Vatican II, Constitution on The Church in the Modern World, 1). The Medellín commitment to work for justice as an essential part of the church's religious mission was echoed in 1971 by the worldwide synod of bishops, which declared such work 'a constitutive dimension of the work of evangelisation'.

This 'new way of being church', as it is sometimes called in Latin America, has attracted immense attention in the church throughout the world – and outside the church as well – for its energy and creativity, and above all for its commitment to changing the inhuman conditions endured by most of Latin America's population. This commitment is illustrated especially by the martyrs, most of them unknown, like the thousands of killed in counter-insurgency campaigns for being associated with base communities, but including two bishops, Bishop Enrique Angelelli of La Rioja in Argentina, murdered by Argentine air force personnel in 1976, and Archbishop Oscar Romero, assassinated on the orders of the Salvadorean oligarchy in 1980.

Though not numerically the majority within the church in Latin America, those Christians who define themselves as in the tradition of Medellín and Puebla have created something new, in the new commitment of bishops, priests and religious and the new confidence of the laity, often uneducated, who discovered that the Word of God in scripture spoke to them and have been able to link their joys and sorrows to the Christian mystery in a wide variety of liturgical forms. This process has been described as a new evangelisation, under way long before the phrase became the official slogan of a conservative restoration in the church.

Medellín also stimulated the flowering of a local church, a beginning of inculturation, to use today's term, a first realisation within the universal church of the diversity within communion heralded by Vatican II. This is another reason for its importance to the universal church, and for the intense interest it has aroused in the church throughout the world. Those dioceses which have implemented Medellín and Puebla have thereby most thoroughly transformed church life in the spirit of Vatican II, in the direction of what Puebla called 'communion and participation'. This explains the hostility it has aroused in powerful circles in the Vatican, which regard Vatican II as having opened the floodgates to undesirable modern ideas which undermine traditional authority. For these people the committed church in Latin America represents the 'threat of a good example'.

The conservative reaction

The change which took place at Medellín horrified many conservatives. The papal delegate to the Medellín conference, Cardinal Antonio Samoré, was so appalled at the direction taken by the bishops that he decided to return to Rome early. While waiting to leave, he retired to his room and refused all contact with the delegates. It was only a determined harangue through his closed door by Bishop Ramón Bogarín of Paraguay that persuaded him to return to the meeting rather than denouncing it in Rome.

Reaction subsequently took a more serious turn. The process of renewal in the Latin American church was initially coordinated and promoted by the Latin American Episcopal Council, usually known as

CELAM, formed in 1955 at the first conference of Latin American bishops in Rio de Janeiro. In 1972 Alfonso López Trujillo, then auxiliary bishop of Bogotá, Colombia, was elected secretary-general of CELAM. López Trujillo was secretary-general of CELAM until 1979 and thereafter president until 1983.

Under his influence, CELAM, which had hitherto promoted the church renewal initiated at Medellín, became a channel for conservative pressures, and the preparations for the Puebla conference were marked by tension between Trujillo, backed by Cardinal Sebastiano Baggio, president of the Pontifical Commission for Latin America and prefect of the powerful Congregation for Bishops, which controls episcopal appointments, and the then president of CELAM, the Brazilian Cardinal Aloísio Lorscheider. The Puebla conference itself was the scene of a vigorous attempt, ultimately unsuccessful, to 'roll back' the theology ratified at Medellín, using the authority of the newly elected Pope John Paul II, whose first journey outside Italy as Pope was to open the Puebla conference.[1] Other prominent figures associated with this movement are Colombian bishop Darío Castrillón Hoyos and Franciscan Bishop Boaventura Kloppenburg, one of the main spokesmen of the conservative Brazilian bishops. Key connections at the Roman end of this network are the Congregation for Bishops and the Pontifical Commission for Latin America.

This trend in policy-making has been accentuated during the pontificate of John Paul II, and the bishops appointed since his election in 1979 have generally been conservative or conformist, making it hard to avoid the conclusion that there is a deliberate policy to change the direction of the Latin American church by changing its leadership. Examples include the appointment of Opus Dei bishops in Peru, where they now exercise a powerful influence on the bishops' conference, and the appointment of a conservative Brazilian priest resident for many years in Rome, José Cardoso Sobrinho, to undo the work of Archbishop Helder Câmara in Recife. Similarly the life's work of Cardinal Arns in São Paulo is being effectively dismantled by the division of the archdiocese.

Another example of this policy has been the Vatican's treatment of the Latin American Confederation of Religious (CLAR). CLAR is one of the few continent-wide bodies in the Latin American church, and faithfully represented the radical commitment of Latin American religious to the poor. In 1989 its bible study programme, *Palabra y Vida* ('Word and Life') was condemned by Rome, and shortly afterwards the Vatican refused to accept CLAR's elected secretary-general; in his place it appointed the Colombian priest, Jorge Jiménez, and subsequently named a Colombian bishop as 'papal delegate', effectively taking the place of the elected chair. When the next elections in CLAR were due, the Vatican suspended the organisation's procedures and appointed its own team.

While John Paul II told the Brazilian bishops in 1986 that liberation theology was 'useful and necessary', and the two Vatican documents devoted to it in 1984 and 1986 were forced to admit that liberation was a fundamental Christian concept, the Vatican authorities have exerted constant pressure on liberation theologians. The most famous example is Leonardo Boff, who decided to resign from the priesthood in 1992 after years of harassment, but there is also constant pressure on seminaries and Catholic universities to toe the Roman line.

II. THE ISSUES FOR SANTO DOMINGO

Fixed as it was to coincide with the quincentenary of Columbus' arrival in the Americas, the Santo Domingo conference was intended to be an occasion for taking stock, not just of the current state of the church, but of its role in the Americas since 1492.

There were in addition new challenges, both socio-economic and religious. The 'new world order' ushered in by the fall of Eastern European state socialism is proving to be as oppressive economically in the countries of the South as any political tyranny. The increased integration of the world economy, coupled with the gospel of free trade (which means no restraints on rich countries in dealing with the poor) leaves even less space for the South: even their raw materials, as well as their people, may now be surplus to the rich world's requirements. Many countries in the continent have emerged from military dictatorship (Brazil) or civil war (El Salvador) to democracies which are still fragile, offering little scope for popular participation and often agents of the economic policies of the international financial institutions: reduced spending on welfare and education, privatisation and opening up local economies even more to foreign competition.

In this situation, the church committed to the poor is still a minority. Paradoxically, it is in danger of being an elite among the poor, restricted to the organised, those who feel able to take responsibility for the wider society. In the cities many people are turning to Pentecostal churches to meet their religious and human needs. Throughout the continent, these questions have been debated. Is the problem a liturgy still too European and intellectual, a church structure which still excludes women from the key leadership positions, which does not recognise African and indigenous traditions, or one which too quickly rejected popular religion?

Such were the questions being asked by the adherents of the 'option for the poor'. Their opponents saw Santo Domingo as an opportunity to reaffirm a more positive, even triumphalist, view of the presence of the church in Latin America, and celebrate the 500 years anniversary. For them the growth of fundamentalist Protestantism – dismissed with the label 'the sects' – was proof that the 'new way of being church' had failed, and that what was needed was a restoration of earlier forms of theology, spirituality and worship, held in place by a tighter church discipline.

III. THE ORGANISATION OF THE SANTO DOMINGO CONFERENCE

As early as the Puebla conference, there had been talk of holding the following conference in 1992 to mark the fifth centenary of the arrival of Christianity in Latin America with Christopher Columbus in 1492. In 1983, in Haiti, Pope John Paul II launched the theme of a 'new evangelisation' and proclaimed a 'novena of years' devoted to reflection and designed to culminate in the Santo Domingo conference.[2]

In view of the conservative views which dominated CELAM, whose president in this period was the Colombian bishop and ally of López Trujillo, Darío Castrillón Hoyos, it is not surprising that the initial formulations of the conference agenda had quite different emphases from what been the dominant approach in the Latin American church since Medellín. The idea of a 'new evangelisation' was taken in a conservative sense, and linked to a concept of 'culture' which had also been used at Puebla in an attempt to empty the option for the poor of its political content. The approach was visible in the theme first suggested for the conference, 'New Evangelisation and New Culture', and a series of preparatory documents issued by CELAM between 1989 and 1990 were dominated by the supposed danger of the disintegration of Latin American culture in the face of an 'incoming culture'. The remedy suggested was a return to 'the Christian substratum of Latin America', by means of a restoration of older models of church authority and discipline.

In December 1990 Pope John Paul II announced the final version of the theme: 'New Evangelisation, Human Promotion: Christian Culture: Jesus Christ Yesterday, Today and Forever', and at the end of April 1991 the final consultation document was distributed at the end of the general assembly of CELAM. Like the earlier drafts, the consultation document stressed the need to rebuild a Christian culture to confront modern pluralism; it also abandoned the priority given to social analysis in the tradition of Medellín and Puebla, the method summarised in the Young Christian Workers formula: 'see, judge, act'.

The production of the consultation document was the last act of the outgoing CELAM executive. The new executive, elected in 1991, was headed by Cardinal Nicolás López Rodríguez, in recognition of the fact that the conference was to be held in his Santo Domingo diocese, with the auxiliary bishop of Brasília, Raymundo Damasceno Assis, as secretary-general.

Complaints soon began to be voiced by the Latin American bishops, not only that the consultation document abandoned the line of Medellín and Puebla, but that it had taken no account of the comments the bishops' conferences had submitted on the previous drafts. To meet these complaints the new CELAM secretary-general ordered the publication of two further documents. The first, known as the *Prima Relatio*, was a compilation of all the submissions from bishops' conferences, and was published in September 1991. The second, the *Secunda Relatio*, published in January 1992, was a synthesis of the views received from bishops' conferences and other church bodies by November 1991. It now became clear that there was a large measure of common ground among the bishops, and that they saw the main challenges to evangelisation, including cultural disintegration, as stemming from economic exploitation and political repression, and the methodology of Medellín and Puebla as the one most appropriate to the Latin American situation.

On the basis of these two documents, a meeting of secretaries of bishops' conferences in February 1992 set the guidelines for the Working

Document for Santo Domingo: it seemed that the views of the Latin American bishops would after all prevail.

The Working Document, drafted in Bogotá and sent to Rome for formal approval, stayed in Rome for two months. This delay meant that its contents were not widely known in Latin America. The Working Document was eventually published, but, in an unprecedented move, it was also announced that a second secretary-general of the Santo Domingo conference had been appointed, Jorge Medina Estévez, an extremely reactionary Chilean bishop and friend of the former Chilean dictator, Augusto Pinochet, well connected in Rome but unpopular with his fellow Chilean bishops. This was the prelude to a total restructuring of the conference.

IV. THE COURSE OF THE CONFERENCE

One of the most potent symbols of the Santo Domingo event itself was the sight of the Pope celebrating mass on the Sunday before the conference opened at the controversial 'Columbus Lighthouse'. This grotesque concrete construction, compared variously to a multi-storey car park and an Aztec altar, was in fact a mausoleum, designed to house what the government of the Dominican Republic claimed to be the bones of Christopher Columbus. The centrepiece of the official Dominican Republic celebrations of the 500 years, the monument was controversial both because it represented a triumphal alliance of church and state rejected by most Latin American bishops, and because to make space for it almost 1,000 families had been evicted from the site. Formally, the 'Lighthouse' had nothing to do with the bishops' conference, but the senior president of the conference, Cardinal Rodríguez of Santo Domingo, was also the president of the official Dominican Republic commission to celebrate the Columbus quincentenary. He denounced critics of the project in the local press as 'loudmouths and layabouts'.

The role of the Dominican primate seemed designed to make the papal mass a celebration of a church-state alliance. All other Sunday masses had been cancelled in Santo Domingo to induce a large attendance, and many of the bishop delegates attended to accompany the Pope, though most of the Brazilians diplomatically arrived later. Dwarfed by the huge monument, the Pope, weak from his recent cancer operation, and uncomfortable with the heat and crowds, attempted to strike a balance between the radical criticism of the 500 years celebration and the blatant triumphalism of the Dominican government and archbishop.

As the conference opened, the fears of a Vatican counter-coup against the brief attempt at genuine consultation which produced the Working Document were confirmed. The standing orders of the conference placed almost total power in the hands of the steering committee or 'presidency', as it was known. This consisted of Cardinal López Rodríguez, Cardinal Angelo Sodano, Vatican secretary of state and former nuncio in Pinochet's Chile, Archbishop Serafim Fernandez, the conservative archbishop of Belo Horizonte in Brazil, and the two secretaries, Bishop Raymundo Damasceno Assis, secretary-general of CELAM, and the unexpectedly appointed Bishop Jorge Medina. Another appointment which attracted comment was that of Fr Jorge Jiménez to be in charge of the 'dynamic' of the conference. Fr Jiménez had been appointed by the Vatican to manage the Latin American Confederation of Religious after the removal of the elected secretary-general, and was to play an important role in interpreting the hermetic regulations of the Santo Domingo conference. The conference opened, as had Puebla, with an address by the Pope, but there was then an innovation: four 'magisterial lectures', one on each of the elements of the theme (christology, 'new evangelisation', 'human promotion', and 'Christian culture') were announced, intended to structure the discussions. It was made clear that the Working Document was no longer relevant.

The official experts proposed by CELAM, who had produced the Working Document, were rejected (except for one, the most conservative) and another group appointed, not including any notable liberation theologians. Among the Vatican's appointed experts were Enrique Iglesias, a former Uruguayan foreign minister and Washington-based head of the Inter-American Development Bank, and Christine Vollmer, the wife of a Venezuelan beer magnate and president of the Latin American Alliance for the Family. Brazilian Bishop Cândido Padin, though elected by his fellow bishops, was excluded, on the ground that he was retired, although he was a member of the executive of the Brazilian Bishops' Conference and president of the Laity Commission (and the laity were supposed to be a key theme at Santo Domingo). It later turned out that at least three other retired bishops had been accepted as delegates, one directly nominated by the Vatican after he had not been elected by his fellow bishops.

On the afternoon of Monday 12 October, the day after the mass at the Columbus monument, Pope John Paul II delivered the inaugural address of the conference. The atmosphere could not have been more different. This was a purely church event, and very much a talk within the family; whatever reservations some bishops might have about the Pope's policies, the atmosphere of respect and affection was palpable.

Described by one bishop as a synthesis of the Pope's teaching during his pontificate, the address presented the familiar features of John Paul's position: the stress on the figure of Christ, followed by repetition of his warning at Puebla on 'reductionist christologies', a strong passage on a view of freedom of conscience and theological pluralism 'carried as far as a relativism which threatens the integrity of the faith' – this passage was delivered in Portuguese, prompting some wry comments. The Pope called – again speaking Portuguese – for base communities to be based on the eucharist and in full union with the local bishop, which might have been taken as criticism, but the fact that they were mentioned at all drew applause from the delegates. The Pope, who appeared tired, was particularly animated when he discussed social issues, thumping the table to reinforce his point. He described the gulf between rich and poor countries, and between rich and poor within countries, as 'a real disorder and institutionalised injustice', and repeated his call in Centesimus Annus for 'a change in mentality, behaviour and structures'. An unexpected element of his speech was a proposal for 'a meeting of representatives of episcopates of the whole American continent, possibly in the form of a synod'. Opinion was divided as to whether this would be a device for diluting the radicalism of the Latin American church by adding northern caution, or whether the ideas which underlay the US bishops' pastoral on economic issues might stiffen the Latin Americans' social concern, but in any case little more was heard of the idea, which was rumoured to be disliked by the curia.

Tension surfaced the following day at the first working session of the conference, without the Pope, when bishops demanded a say in the composition of the various committees, especially the coordinating committees and the drafting committee, responsible for producing the final text. There were calls for the 'magisterial lectures' to be dropped. The most these representations achieved was that the presidents declared that they had 'taken account' of the views of the assembly in nominating the various commissions; in Puebla these had been elected by the delegates. What was widely regarded as the only positive result of this process was the appointment of the president of the Brazilian Bishops' Conference, Archbishop Luciano Mendes de Almeida, as the chair of the drafting committee, and he was indeed to play a crucial role in the shaping of the final document.

Another motive for initial frustration was the arrangements for the delegates' accommodation. The delegates were housed in luxury hotels in various parts of the capital, in national groups, except that cardinals were all placed together, and the curial representatives in a different hotel. The separation made it difficult for the bishops to make informal contacts and slowed down the process by which the conference acquired an identity and *esprit de corps*. The style of accommodation led a group of bishops to ask if simpler accommodation could be found. By then it was too late, and the conference organisers dismissed the request as gesture politics, 'playing at being poor', in the words of Bishop Castrillón.

Two other incidents exemplified what was felt as the arrogance of the conference managers. At the end of the first week 33 Brazilian bishops, with widespread support, proposed that the conference should celebrate a penitential liturgy asking pardon for the abuses committed during the previous 500 years, especially the suffering inflicted on the indigenous population and the Africans brought as slaves to America. The president of the next session, on Monday morning, Cardinal López Rodríguez, instead of calling the proposer of the motion to speak in its support, called the Argentine Bishop Italo Di Stefano, who criticised 'a guilt complex which might lessen the zeal of the new evangelisation'. Cardinal López informed the assembly that the presidency had received many criticisms of the proposal on the grounds that such an expression of contrition might lend itself to ideological manipulation. With that, and without a vote, the matter was dropped. This behaviour took on a different light two days later, when it was learned that the Pope, at a regular audience in Rome, had asked forgiveness for the abuses of the past, but the Dominican primate persisted in his hostility to any expression of contrition on the part of the church, refusing to allow the cathedral to be used for a penitential celebration and trying to prevent any bishops from attending the service organised a week later by the base communities of Santo Domingo; in the end two Brazilians attended.

When the bishops' regular morning liturgy was devoted to this theme several days later, Cardinals López Rodríguez and Sodano were both absent.

The second incident came with the announcement that Guatemalan indigenous leader Rigoberta Menchú had been awarded the Nobel Peace Prize. While the news was applauded by the conference, Cardinal Arns' proposal that the conference should send an official message of congratulations was not put to the vote, on the same ground that it could be misused for ideological purposes, and in the end the Guatemalan bishops sent their own message.

One comment widely quoted summed up the irritation of many bishops: 'It isn't a bishops' conference; it's a conference for bishops.' But frustration was not the whole story. There was evident pleasure among the bishops at the opportunity to meet other bishops of the continent, something which CELAM has not encouraged in recent years. This took time, especially since the delegates were scattered round Santo Domingo, but the contacts produced, not just a feeling of camaraderie, but a sense of a shared Latin American church tradition, reinforced by the blatant attempts to manipulate the conference. This may well be the most important result of Santo Domingo, especially if it has the result that CELAM becomes more representative of the continent's bishops.

The course of the conference also broke down some of the stereotypes of radicals and conservatives. The Brazilians, as the largest delegation, used to conference procedures from the meetings of their own 300-strong assembly, were one of the most vigorous forces for more openness, but this attitude was shared by the Guatemalan and Bolivian delegations, and by bishops from almost every country. The Venezuelan bishops, not normally regarded as progressive, were vehemently critical of the abstract christology of the final document.

Outside the conference hall there were various events which represented the reality of the Latin American church better than the battles inside. One was the visits paid by some of the bishops on the first Sunday of the conference to celebrate the liturgy with local communities. On one of these Cardinal Arns presided at a mass before a crowd gathered under the trees of the churchyard to escape the heat. All sang the Nicaraguan *Misa Campesina*, which sees Jesus as a carpenter, plumber and petrol pump attendant, and describes his execution at the hands of the 'Roman imperialists'. At the offertory the people brought up a picture

15

of Archbishop Romero, a painting of 'Our Lady of Latin America' in a pose reminiscent of Boadicea, and a family evicted by a local businessman.

A similar 'liberated zone' was created by the daily briefings organised by a team of Latin American journalists in the basement of Cardinal Sodano's hotel. In addition to a regular bulletin analysing the significance of developments in the conference, the group laid on talks by leading Latin American Catholic intellectuals on the background issues to the conference; towards the end of the conference some bishops also gave talks. Their work enabled journalists to pool information and get a sense of the context of the conference discussions, a very important contribution, as many of the journalists had only a sketchy acquaintance with the role of the church in Latin America. At one of these press conferences representatives of base communities in Santo Domingo gave an example of the fundamental loyalty they have to the church and its leaders: the Pope, they said, looked sad at the mass at the Columbus mausoleum because he could not see the poor. These alternative briefings were all the more necessary because of the lack of information provided by the official conference. Frustrated by being served up a succession of apparatchiks or nonentities at the daily press briefings, over 60 journalists signed a petition to the press office asking to be allowed to hear the 'prophetic voices' of Cardinal Arns, Cardinal Lorscheider, Bishop Flores of Guatemala and Archbishop Luna of Ecuador, among others. The press office acceded, and subsequent press conferences included a notably more representative selection of delegates, including Cardinal Arns and Bishop Flores.

None of Latin America's best known theologians had been appointed as an official adviser to the conference. Some bishops' conferences brought their own experts, but the most creative minds in Latin American theology were reduced to operating more or less underground, squeezed into a religious house in a quiet street near the conference hall, communicating by electronic mail with a back-up team in Mexico and keeping in touch with friendly bishops inside the conference hall by mobile phone. If at times the clandestinity seemed exaggerated, it was yet one more indication of the attitude engendered among Latin American theologians – most of whom depend on church institutions for their livelihood – by the harassment to which they are subjected by the Roman authorities.

The position of these theologians was in marked contrast to the position of three priests who were also not official advisers but were given a key role in the drafting of the final texts: Maximinio Arias Riyero, a Spanish priest living in Chile and close to Bishop Medina, who monitored the drafting on behalf of the co-secretary of the conference, Octavio Ruiz, a Colombian priest on the staff of the Congregation for the Doctrine of the Faith in Rome, who drafted the final version of the christological section, and Josep-Ignasi Saranyana, of Opus Dei, who produced the final version of the historical section.

The various devices used by CELAM and the Roman curia to restrict debate at Santo Domingo had precedents at Puebla. The preparations had followed a similar course, there was a similar proportion of Vatican-nominated delegates, and no liberation theologians had been officially invited. At Puebla, however, individual bishops and bishops' conferences invited liberation theologians to be on hand for consultation, and their presence was widely known. At Puebla the bishops rejected the schema proposed by the conference organisers, and adopted a methodology which made the lived situation of Latin Americans, rather than doctrinal reflection, the basis of their discussions. At Santo Domingo, in contrast, the assembly was never able to achieve full control of its proceedings, and there was a war of attrition between a large group of bishops and the conference organisers which lasted throughout the conference.

Confusion, tension, crisis

On the fourth day of the conference, the bishops began work in 30 thematic commissions, each studying a particular issue. The membership of the commissions was determined by the presidency, 'taking into account' the wishes of the bishop delegates, an opaque procedure that caused some irritation among the bishops. In some cases the resulting groups showed signs of having been carefully balanced to prevent undesirable statements emerging, and in some cases conflicts almost brought the commissions' work to a standstill.

The commission on the religious life included Cardinal Somalo, from the Vatican Congregation for Religious, Cardinal Landázuri from Peru, Bishop López Hurtado from Colombia, who had been the 'papal delegate' appointed by the Vatican to manage CLAR after its constitution was suspended, two polar opposites from Brazil, the liberal Archbishop Luciano Mendes Almeida and the conservative Bishop Karl Romer, Bishop Domingo Salvador from Peru and Augusto Vargas from Argentina and among the non-episcopal members Fr Marcial Maciel, superior general of the Legionaries of Christ. Discussion in this commission was minimal, with a few members dominating, and the first drafts led to a letter to the presidency signed by a majority the religious taking part in the conference complaining about the procedure and suggesting an alternative text.

The commission on ecumenism was also tense. The non-Catholic observers withdrew at one point, after it had been suggested that their presence might constrain discussion on some topics, and had to be heavily persuaded to return. At one point a parallel commission on ecumenism was established, including Brazilian Bishop Boaventura Kloppenburg, one of the rapporteurs of the official commission, until it was dissolved by the presidency after protests from the official commission

In other cases the commissions represented the main space of freedom for the delegates, where they could determine the subjects and the method of discussion. The work of the commissions was hampered, however, first by unclarity about what sort of document they were producing, since the Working Document had been silently jettisoned, and then by the 'magisterial lectures', which not only interrupted the meetings of the commissions, but were generally regarded as unhelpful and out of key with Latin American theological method. The final problem came when the contributions of these thematic commissions were passed on to the drafting committee. As the Brazilian observer put it, 'The work of the thematic commissions was largely abandoned by the drafting committee, which insisted on its schemas. The one exception was the section on human promotion, where it was possible to restore much of the commissions' text.' The simple reason for this was that the final editing of the chapter on human promotion was done by a sub-group headed by Archbishop Luciano Mendes, while the other sections were edited by other sub-groups, the christology section in particular being tightly supervised by Bishop Jorge Medina. The thematic commissions were dissolved on Wednesday 21 October, and it then became much more difficult for the bishops to exercise control over the text. At this point, the bishops' trust in Archbishop Luciano Mendes was skilfully manipulated by Bishop Medina, whose assumption of greater authority than his colleague as secretary, Bishop Damasceno Assis, the permanent secretary-general of CELAM, was widely noted. On 16 October, the fifth day of the conference, Archbishop Mendes had secured the delegates' approval for the general structure of the document, but this 'indicative vote' was used on several occasions by Bishop Medina to reject amendments to the text produced by the drafting committee.

Despite the tight control, the bishops' rejected the drafting committee's text on the 500 years and severely criticised the profession of faith. It was at this point that drafts ceased to be submitted for approval by the plenary, and a request was made for amendments only. This was seen by many bishops as a severe weakening of the assembly's control over the text.

The Thursday of the second week, 22 October, was the crisis point of the conference. Delegates had received the first draft of the complete final document two days before, and were extremely unhappy. The text was criticised on all sides as wordy, boring and containing no new ideas; the Argentine bishops were particularly vehement. The conference agenda was suspended, and bishops conferred and caucused in the conference hall for half an hour. Archbishop Luciano Mendes finally asked the conference for 'a sort of blessing' to enable work to continue, promising that more account would be taken of the conclusions of the thematic commissions. The resulting vote called for 'a shorter and more concentrated text'.

Unfortunately, when the revised version appeared, the cuts had been drastic: in particular the chapter on human promotion had been cut by half. This draft appeared only two days before the end of the conference, and efforts to amend it meant that voting went on until shortly before the closing liturgy. Five thousand amendments were submitted, and, thanks to the cooperation of Archbishop Luciano Mendes, the chapter on human promotion was restored to the form given it by the commissions. Other sections of the text fared differently. On the last morning Cardinal Sodano successfully threw his prestige as 'Secretary of State of his Holiness' behind a sentence declaring that 'The religious of Latin America renew their loyalty to the Pope,' which many bishops (and the drafting committee) had felt unnecessary and inappropriate. After the votes on the amendments, the cardinal gave an undertaking that he would try to secure papal approval for the document in two weeks, instead of the six weeks required in the case of the Puebla document. He concluded: 'Objectives have been achieved. Thanks be to God.' This was glossed by a number of delegates as 'Thank God my objectives have been achieved. I'm going home with the document I planned and wanted; there will be no problem about its approval by the Pope.'

The whole process was summed up by Bishop Demétrio Valentini, chair of the Brazilian bishops' social commission, as one of discontinuity: CELAM's 1991 consultative document was rejected by the Latin American bishops, whose views, synthesised in the *Secunda Relatio*, formed the basis of the Working Document. The Working Document was then abandoned by the conference managers, and the bishops were forced to produce a new text in the 30 commissions. The commissions' text was then largely rejected by the drafting committee. Dissatisfaction with the procedure was also evident in an interview given by the president of the Guatemalan bishops' conference, Bishop Gerardo Flores, in early 1993:

> At times I felt uncomfortable because the procedures were not always clear and there was very little opportunity to express one's views in public. I worked more freely and more happily in the group I was assigned to.... All of us in the group were very pleased with our contribution, although, when it was summarised in the final text, it was heavily mutilated. Nevertheless the clear and precise contributions we had made were not lost.[3]

V. THE SANTO DOMINGO DOCUMENT

The Vatican changes

Vatican control of the conference did not end with the bishops' final vote on their text. As it did with the Puebla document, the Vatican made changes to the bishops' text, many fewer than with Puebla, perhaps because Santo Domingo was under much tighter Roman control.[4]

The first Roman change touches on this very point. The fathers of Santo Domingo described themselves as 'the bishops of the church in Latin America and the Caribbean gathered in Santo Domingo in their Fourth General Conference'. Rome, presumably the Pontifical Commission for Latin America, has changed this to 'the bishops participating in the Fourth General Conference of the Latin American Episcopate', a much weaker concept which seems to remove the idea that this is the

20

teaching of the churches of a region. Oddly, the Caribbean bishops are also written out of Santo Domingo by this change.

There are various changes which have the effect of softening commitments of the conference. The bishops said the new evangelisation should 'proclaim without equivocation the Gospel of justice'; Rome expanded the last phrase into 'the Gospel of justice, love and mercy'. Many of the changes affect references to women. Where the conference called for 'a rethinking of the role of women in the church and pastoral work', Rome has produced a blander formula: 'a deeper reflection on the role of women in church and society'. Here the suggestion that women should have a role in pastoral work disappears, as did a suggestion in one of the early drafts that women should take part in the formation of priests 'as fellow disciples and teachers'. Rome did not like the bishops' recommendation that scriptural exegesis should '*abandon anachronistic interpretations which demean women*' and 'develop a reading of the Word of God which, *from a women's perspective*, reveals the characteristics which women's vocation contributes to the plan of salvation'. The two italicised phrases were removed. References to women having a role in salvation seemed to provoke deep suspicion in Rome. This even affected the Santo Domingo text on land. The bishops described 'two opposed attitudes to land', the first that of Amerindians: 'Land, within the whole set of elements which make up the indigenous community, is life, a sacred place, "the feminine face of God", the integrating centre of the community's life', the second the view of land only as a commodity for making money; they then outlined a Christian view. Rome said that the first two attitudes, that is, including that of the indigenous, are 'both different from the Christian vision', thus closing a door the bishops had left open, and deleted the phrase 'the feminine face of God'.

There is a petty and pedestrian feel to the changes. One even produces absurdity when it makes the document proclaim: 'The church, in proclaiming the gospel, is not usurping a task foreign to its mission,' where the original had 'in proclaiming the gospel of human rights', which Rome apparently objected to.

Santo Domingo and the Latin American tradition

The Santo Domingo final document divides into three parts, of which the second is the most substantial, divided into three chapters, reflecting the official theme of the conference: 'New Evangelisation, Human Promotion, Christian Culture'. The full outline is as follows:

Part I: Jesus Christ, Gospel of the Father
1. Profession of faith
2. The 500 years

Part II: Jesus Christ the Evangeliser, Alive in His Church
1. The new evangelisation
2. Human promotion
3. Christian culture

Part III: Jesus Christ, Life and Hope of Latin America and the Caribbean
Pastoral guidelines

The structure of the document follows much more closely the agenda imposed at Santo Domingo than the Working Document which came out of the consultation process. The section which most closely reflects the views of the bishops is Part II, Chapter 2, on human promotion. As the Brazilian bishops' spokesman put it:

> The chapters are very uneven, and this is not simply a personal judgment, but an objective fact: some reflect much more than others the work of the thematic commissions. The obvious example is that of the chapter on Human Promotion. The fact reveals an important criterion to be understood: some members of the drafting commission did not accept alternative versions proposed in amendments, while others did.
>
> It is worth insisting on this. The chapter on Human Promotion represents much better the work done by the Santo Domingo Conference. In it we can find the world we live in, but we can also find a better expression of our theology, which is present in an integrated way in the various parts of the chapter. You could say that the Conference would have been worthwhile for this chapter alone.

The basis for this limited success is that while the spiritualising theological straitjacket imposed on the bishops was frustrating, it could not in the end conceal the real life of the church in Latin America, though it did restrict its expression. On the other hand, the chapter on human promotion is more than a list of practical resolutions, and is an example of the theological method pioneered in Latin America. Thus the document repeatedly reaffirms its acceptance of the commitments made at Medellín and Puebla, especially 'a preferential option for the poor, deriving from the gospel, which is firm and irrevocable' (178).

22

The bishops identify a series of 'new signs of the times', starting with awareness of human rights, which they describe as deriving from the image of God in which human beings were created, confirmed and perfected in Christ. 'Any violation of human rights contradicts God's Plan and is a sin' (164). The church proclaims 'the gospel of human rights' as an 'essential demand of its evangelising mission' (165).[5] Next, ecology is given extended treatment, starting from the Genesis image of the Spirit hovering over the void at the creation, 'God's first covenant with us' (169). An ecological ethics, say the bishops, 'implies the abandonment of a utilitarian and individualistic morality. It postulates the acceptance of the principle of the universal destiny of all created goods and the promotion of justice and solidarity as essential values.' Starting from the same principle, the document then challenges the idea that land is nothing but a commodity, and contrasts this with its sacred status in indigenous communities.

On more general political and economic issues, the bishops commit themselves to 'proclaim insistently to civil society the values of a genuine democracy which is pluralist, just and participatory' (193). On economics, they echo the Pope's plea for ways of 'reducing, deferring or abolishing' the foreign debt (197), but the bulk of their consideration is given to the inadequacy of the currently dominant neo-liberal approach, 'which goes beyond the purely economic field and derives from narrow or reductionist interpretations of the person and society' (199).

In the chapter on 'Christian culture' the bishops succeed in pulling the discussion away from a simplistic yearning to restore older 'Christian values'. The 'cultural crisis' is defined in one paragraph as meaning political and economic corruption, impunity, inequality and damage to the environment (233). This chapter also contains an important section on the indigenous, Afro-American and mestizo communities, and notes that one goal of 'inculturation' is 'the salvation and integral liberation of a particular people or human group' (244). It accepts that Latin America and the Caribbean form 'a multi-ethnic and pluri-cultural continent'. It says that 'black slavery and the massacres of Indians were the greatest sin of Western colonial expansion', and admits that 'churchmen' were 'not unconnected' with slavery, racism and discrimination. The commitments to support indigenous and black groups in their quest for equality and recognition of their distinct identity are strong and detailed. There is also a section which draws attention to the challenges the church faces in the cities of Latin America.

In a brief final summary of 'priority pastoral directions' the bishops appeal to the pastoral tradition of Vatican II, Medellín and Puebla. Echoing Vatican II, they stress that the particular churches of the continent share 'the joys and the hopes, the griefs and anxieties' of their peoples, and note that the implementation of Santo Domingo has to be carried out by 'each particular church and each episcopal conference'. The commitments of this section are expressed in one paragraph in terms which could stand with any from the previous conferences:

> We make our own the cry of the poor. We adopt with renewed zeal the gospel's preferential option for the poor, in continuity with Medellín and Puebla. This option, which is neither exclusive nor excluding, will enlighten, in imitation of Jesus Christ, all our activity of evangelisation. Thus enlightened, we invite all to promote a new economic, social and political order, befitting the dignity of each and every person, pressing for justice and solidarity and opening to all horizons of eternity (296).

In contrast, the earlier sections of the document abandon the 'see-judge-act' methodology of Latin American theology, which was used at Medellín and Puebla, that is, look at the reality of the situation, reflect in faith and plan a response.

Because of this, the Jesus of Part I is hieratic and authoritarian, remote from the Jesus followed in the communities of Latin America. An attempt was made to substitute an alternative, 'an Emmaus christology', in which Jesus' approach to human beings is analysed in terms of the story of the disciples on the road to Emmaus, but this was ruled out of order on the grounds that the bishops had already approved the text in principle, which many bishops saw as a further exercise in manipulation.

The chapter on the church sees the primary need to restore the church to holiness, doctrine and discipline, but these are seen as other-worldly, intellectual and authoritarian. So greater instruction is called for, and base communities are to be made cells of the parish, rather than 'a new way of being church'. An example of the tension in this area was a ping-pong process between the bishops and theological revisers: the revisers persisted in deleting the word 'base' from the standard expression 'church base communities', because of its supposed political implications, and the bishops steadfastly restored it. The activity of the church, following from the vision of Christ, is seen as fundamentally hieratic, cultic, not in the world. This even affects the calls for social action, where the Vatican changed the bishops' text, which had called for the church to be involved in work for human rights. The altered version reads: 'pastors must encourage the laity to be involved'.

One of the striking features of the document is the way it largely ignores the distinctive achievements of the Latin American church since Medellín. It certainly does not celebrate them. In fact, the main place where the document is enthusiastic about the church is when it is making propaganda points about the church's role in the 16th century, arguing, for example, that the church was always on the side of the Indians. There is nothing on Archbishop Romero, and only a cursory reference to people who have given their lives (who are significantly not called martyrs). When key aspects of church life in Latin America are mentioned, such as the rediscovery of the bible or base communities, it is mainly to point out their limitations.

The reception of Santo Domingo

Contrary to a widespread belief, even in the Roman Catholic Church the relation between teaching and faith is one of dialogue. Teaching has to be 'received'. '1993 is the year of the reception of Santo Domingo,' said one Brazilian bishop. The Brazilian bishops will stress the role of the laity and the need for inculturation, 'macro-ecumenism', relations with non-Christian religions; for them these are the new things that come out of Santo Domingo. In addition, a number of bishops' conferences are taking care to place Santo Domingo in the context of Vatican II, Medellín and Puebla, and so interpret it in the light of this tradition. This is in fact what happened with the Puebla text, since there are many elements of Puebla which conflict with the tradition of Medellín. A number of bishops' conferences are also using their preparatory materials for the conference, and the *Secunda Relatio*, arguably the most representative synthesis of the views of the Latin American bishops, alongside the conference document in their follow-up.

One of the hopes expressed by many bishops after Santo Domingo is that the meeting had produced a new sense of Latin American identity, sharpened by resentment at the tactics of the conference organisers, a resentment which went beyond the ranks of the progressives. Immediately after Santo Domingo the Chilean bishops rejected candidates favoured by the joint secretary of the conference, Jorge Medina, and elected a progressive president; at least this was not a vote of confidence in Medina. The limitations of local church autonomy were shown soon afterwards, however, when Bishop Medina was made archbishop of Valparaíso. A CELAM council meeting in early 1993 voted to 'clarify' the relationship between CELAM and the Pontifical Commission for Latin America; this is being interpreted as a desire for greater autonomy.

An idea of what the curial organisers would like to have happened was given in the November 1992 issue of *Thirty Days*, the magazine associated with the movement *Comunione e Liberazione*. 'Thirty years of options in Latin America came to an end,' the magazine claims. It quotes Cardinal Sodano, Vatican secretary of state and one of the presidents of the conference, as saying, 'The method the Latin American episcopate has been using for so many years was abandoned: the method of "seeing, judging and acting"... In this conference the dominion of sociological analysis was ended and priority given to proclaiming Christ.' Cardinal Sodano paints a picture of serene harmony among bishops united by the teaching of John Paul II. That this was not the whole story is indicated diplomatically by the president of the Guatemalan bishops' conference, in the interview previously mentioned:

> The presence of so many members of the Roman Curia can be taken as a very great support for our discussions. Some people may also see it as a sign of concern with the orthodoxy and fidelity of the Latin American church, and of the need for a certain control to avoid doctrinal deviations or splits.... Among the cardinals and other participants there were some who really revealed the loving face of the church.... It was perhaps less pleasant and justifiable to have some priests, second-rank employees of the Roman congregations, who wanted a very active role and complicated things.

While the *Thirty Days* article is worthless as an account of events at Santo Domingo, it is a further piece of evidence of a desire in the Vatican to roll back the church of Medellín and Puebla. How far this will succeed is open to question. Very similar tactics were used at Puebla, without notable success, since the ideas and pastoral practice based on the option for the poor are widely felt in Latin America to be the most authentically Christian and most appropriate response to the conditions of the continent. On the other hand, since Puebla the policy of conservative episcopal appointments and pressure on teachers of theology has intensified. The result may be an exodus of the most creative members of the church, or a shift to a position out of reach of clerical power. Leonardo Boff's decision may be the first of many. It would be ironic if the Vatican unwittingly pushed the church towards a declericalised and more pluralist form, although the suffering and loss involved in this process should not be underestimated.

Notes

[1] See Julian Filochowski, 'Medellin to Puebla', *Reflections on Puebla*, CIIR, London, 1980, pp.9-21.

[2] Some of the detail in this and the following section comes from Washington Uranga, *Para Interpretar Santo Domingo*, Centro Nazaret, Buenos Aires, 1992.

[3] *Voces del Tiempo*, Guatemala City, January-March 1993, p.42.

[4] The official English version of the Santo Domingo document is published as *Santo Domingo: Conclusions*, United States Catholic Conference, Washington DC, and CAFOD and CIIR, London, 1993.

[5] The Vatican made this statement nonsense by its alteration. See above, p.21.

The Winds of Santo Domingo and the Evangelisation of Culture

I. SANTO DOMINGO AS AN EVENT

In this article I want to think about Santo Domingo from a particular point of view – as an event with the potential to evangelise culture. I do not deny the need to analyse it from other viewpoints, and in particular, to analyse the text produced by the bishops. But here I concentrate on the event itself, because I believe that simply as an event, it has its own meaning and power to shape our world in various ways. I shall analyse this event in detail later, but first here are a few remarks to explain the title and object of this essay.

Santo Domingo was an event made up of many elements, the most important of which were the preparatory work, the greater or lesser participation in this of all the members of the Latin American church, the texts produced during this period, the Vatican's measures and reactions, and of course, everything that happened at Santo Domingo: the Pope's presence and speeches, the bishops' presence, their declarations and personal positions, also absences and the reasons for them, discussions, tensions and agreements in the hall, celebrations, the various drafts of the text, the final text, its interpretation and reception...

All these elements come together in a text but in themselves they are more than the written text, or rather, they are a text in action, which may even come to have more impact than the one approved by the Pope. This impact is caused by what was said and done during the whole process, what was not said or done, and the way of saying and doing it. So we must take all this into account when speaking of Santo Domingo, even though one element may have more relevance than another, whether it should or not. All this – not just the text – is transmitted to the church and society through what I metaphorically call the 'winds' that drove the process and those the process itself unleashed. Hence the article's title. The point I want to make is that these 'winds' are what may or may not inspire ideals, promote action, and shape the collective awareness in one way or another.

Of course this is nothing new; it has always happened. Important events always generate a text and a spirit – literally, 'winds' – and both influence history. Each does so in its own way, but I think that when the events are relatively recent, the 'spirit' of an event has more influence on the church and society than the 'text' itself. Keeping to our wind metaphor, the 'music' lingers longer than the 'score' – except of course for the experts whose job it is to analyse and transmit this score.

We may take the example of two very important events. Few people today remember the texts of Vatican II, but its refreshing breeze still lingers. In an unincarnate, authoritarian church, that was closed in upon itself, that condemned practically everything that was not itself, that was racked with anxiety and a source of endless anxiety to its faithful because it saw sin everywhere, a miracle occurred. The church opened its doors and windows, it replaced fear by hope, imposition by dialogue, dogmatism by honest debate. Of course the Council's texts should be analysed and the correct interpretation of them can be discussed indefinitely, as is happening now. But even today I believe that the Council's spirit of openness, dialogue, freedom, hope, compassion and returning to Jesus is more important than its texts, however important they may be. And if these texts continue to be significant and meaningful today it is because, although some were better than others, they were imbued as a whole with this spirit.

Likewise with Medellín. Again, few people are familiar with its texts today. And among those who are, there are some who say that Puebla and even Santo Domingo have better texts than Medellín. And in a sense they are right. Nevertheless, I do not think that the spirit of Medellín has been surpassed and it is this spirit that holds on – against wind and tide – to the fundamental: that we must go out to the poor of this world, become incarnate in them, defend them and take risks for them, denounce their oppressors. This is the way the church becomes the church of Jesus, and Christians become followers of Jesus and believers in his God.

In spite of 'antiquated' texts, Medellín is still the unsurpassed symbol of the 'new' evangelisation. Its spirit – and not just this or that text – is what caused the most radical change in the Latin American church from its beginning and what worked the miracle that made this church become Christian and Latin American for the first time in its history.

My second preliminary reflection is on another tack, but it is suggested and even forced upon us by Santo Domingo's central theme: the new evangelisation, or more specifically, the evangelisation of cultures. This can be understood in various ways: either as the adaptation of the faith to different cultures, or as the shaping of any culture in accordance with Christian values and formulations. Here I want to look at the subject of evangelising culture from another perspective.

To put it simply, we may ask what air we humans breathe, and whether it is pure or contaminated. We may consider that our atmosphere is full of lies and deceit, cruelty and injustice, hybris and pride, so that –structurally – our culture predisposes us towards evil, and not towards good. We may consider that this contamination is destroying the ecology not only of the body but also of the spirit. If this is so, evangelising the culture means introducing integrity, kindness, generosity, justice and dignity into it...

Important historical events must also be analysed from this viewpoint, and so we must ask whether Santo Domingo, as an event, evangelised our world or not. Did it help to purify or contaminate our atmosphere? In answering these questions we must remember that we never start with a clean slate. Like Jesus we have to announce the good news in the presence of evil realities and in opposition to them. We have to announce God's kingdom in the presence of the anti-kingdom ruled by idols and in opposition to them. So when we analyse Santo Domingo we have to determine whether it evangelised the culture, the air we breathe, or not, whether in doing this or that, it confronted the powerful. And I repeat, this may be expressed in texts, but goes beyond them.

So from this perspective I am going to ask, as objectively as possible, the following question: how and how much did Santo Domingo evangelise the world we live in? How helpful was it for putting into practice the formulations of faith it requires of us and the texts it offers us?

II. SANTO DOMINGO AS AN EVANGELISING EVENT

1. Latin American identity and Roman imposition

In the preparatory document called the *Secunda Relatio*, drawn up by the Latin American bishops in their own dioceses, we read this splendid text that can stand as a summary of what is new and special and best in the Latin American church since Vatican II:

> On 24 March 1980 the church and world opinion were appalled by the horrible murder of the Archbishop of El Salvador, Oscar Arnulfo Romero, who fell riddled with bullets while celebrating mass, a martyr to the episcopal ministry because he acted like a prophet.
>
> Nearly ten years later in the same city of San Salvador on the night of November 16th 1989, six Jesuit priests of the Central American University, together with two women domestic workers, were cruelly massacred in their home by soldiers during the curfew. The news again shook the world: they died for their commitment as priests and religious to justice and respect for human rights and their ministerial option for the young and the poor.
>
> These facts, together with many other examples, show that in recent decades our church in Latin America has become a church of martyrs and persecuted Christians. In the galaxy of murdered martyrs, together with bishops, priests, seminarians, monks and nuns, there are a large majority of lay pastoral agents, peasants and workers. Others have been attacked, kidnapped, tortured and exiled.
>
> What is historically new about this persecution is its context. It is happening within the western Christian church and perpetrated by those who claim to be defenders of this culture and Christian principles. It is happening because the various idolatries oppressing the Continent, which were denounced at Puebla, have felt threatened by the Church since Medellín and Puebla, and have tried to combat it in various ways: by the spreading and financing of sects propounding a spiritualistic and uncommitted religiosity, by supporting a liberal individualistic Christianity and also by direct attack and persecution.
>
> In the present day situation in Latin America, this is how the Church, faithful to its faith in the God of life and its mission of salvation and liberation, bears witness through persecution and martyrdom.

Not even the faintest echo of this important text remains in the final document of Santo Domingo. I shall return to it later, but now I want to ask the reason for such a notable omission. In our opinion – except in matters of detail – the reason is Roman imposition upon a Latin

American church that was beginning to acquire its own evangelical identity. This is my starting point for this analysis.

There is authoritarianism in all societies, and also centralism if we look at the world as a whole. This involves submission to superpowers. Others in their turn promote dialogue, really 'democratic' attitudes, which, to use political language, come close to the fraternal relations required of us by the gospel. This problem also appeared in what was done – rather than in the theoretical discussion about it – at Santo Domingo, and more blatantly than at Medellín or Puebla. The fact is that, in spite of denials and euphemisms, there was not only diversity and pluralism at the conference but strong tension, that could not be concealed, between the Vatican and certain bishops who supported its line on the one hand, and a large majority of Latin American bishops on the other.

This particular tension went far beyond differences of ideological and theological positions. The form it took was the clear imposition by the Vatican on the conference, unlike what happened at Medellín and Puebla. The Vatican imposed the three presidents of the assembly – all with well known conservative records. It controlled the drafting committee, it reversed the traditional 'see-judge-act' procedure in the preparation of texts so that it became 'judge-see-act'. (We shall come back to this because what is at issue is much more than a change in the word order.) It prevented the excellent *Secunda Relatio* document, and even the more moderate Working Document, from really being used as the basis for discussion. In addition, on important and symbolically significant occasions there was obvious tension between the presidency and the assembly. One of these occasions was the mass asking for forgiveness, which the first two presidents did not attend. Another was the request that the assembly should formally send a letter congratulating Rigoberta Menchú, who had just received the Nobel Peace Prize. This request was refused by the presidency, on the grounds that the assembly's letter might be ideologically manipulated.

These and many other incidents show, beyond any possibility of concealment, the tension between the Vatican and the Latin American church. This tension is certainly nothing new. It came out in the 1984 and 1986 Vatican instructions on liberation theology, in the Vatican intervention in the Latin American Confederation of Religious (CLAR), and in general, in the Vatican policy of episcopal appointments, whose result is that the generation of bishops with whom we will go into the next century will be very different from that of Medellín.

Santo Domingo was no exception. The Latin American bishops as a whole did not appear to regard servility as a good thing – though they accept responsible obedience – and they were less easily manipulated than the presidency hoped. This was revealed in many discussions and votes in the conference hall and in statements made outside it. But in the end they had to bow to Vatican demands. In method, in key committees and in the basic theological direction, most of them had to yield to Vatican pressure.

This authoritarianism and centralism do the church no good. Inside the church communion becomes much more difficult in fact – although this highest expression of the church's mystery has recently been promoted in many Vatican admonitions. Neither fellowship nor the freedom of the sons and daughters of God are reflected in this behaviour. As for the Santo Domingo assembly itself, the Vatican imposition was not only clearly in evidence from the beginning, but even determined the course taken by the assembly, wasting a great deal of energy, which could have been better employed in drafting a decent text. Worst of all, it sent a sad message to the local churches, never mind the marginalised: fear of freedom and creativity, fear of looking at reality or even God from a different point of view, that of the marginalised; in these churches it inculcated a fear of being themselves.

From the viewpoint of the evangelisation of culture, it is encouraging on the one hand that the bishops of the periphery, simply and firmly refused to be imposed upon by the centre. On the other hand, the atmosphere of imposition and the real imposition that occurred at Santo Domingo was a lost opportunity to evangelise a world that is very keen on authoritarianism and centralism. For example, it was a lost opportunity to tell the powers of the North, the UN and international bodies, that they should welcome, respect and encourage voices from outside and not – as nearly always happens – impose upon them what is to be done.

I have begun with this point in order to be honest about the situation, but also because this tension between Roman imposition and Latin American creativity dominated the conference and made it not only ambivalent – with, in theory, two poles: hierarchy and base – but in fact ambiguous. It put a full stop – for now – to the whole process surrounding

Santo Domingo. It means we must be bold and decisive in order to put into practice what is best in the text. We cannot count on a favourable wind from the Vatican.

But, finally, there is a positive aspect to this. There was imposition, many hours were spent in arguments and fights, but this means that the Latin American church does have an identity, Medellín is not dead. Today this church does not enjoy a favourable wind, but it is still there. Attempts will be made to neutralise it through bureaucratic means, but pastoral work, theology, preaching the gospel and faith itself can still count on that identity. It is sad that it had to appear *sub specie contrarii*, as resistance to imposition. But it did appear and it can be put to work.

2. Seriously asking forgiveness

History – the fifth centenary – and geography – Santo Domingo, the former island of Hispaniola – required the church to say something about what happened then and during these past five centuries. The location demanded that a decision should be taken on whether or not to ask the surviving indigenous people for forgiveness, since whole races and peoples, religions and cultures became extinct, or were wiped out by the conquistadors. And whether to ask forgiveness from the black people brought from Africa, as merchandise in a disgraceful trade, one of the worst and most brutal crimes in history.

There is no doubt whatever, even without resorting to black legends, that an immense sin against humanity was perpetrated, which became an original sin and the origin of further sin. Asking forgiveness for this sin is indispensable for evangelising the culture and purifying the poisonous air, which covers up the crime with arrogance and is thick with contempt for the 'other'. Neither governments, nor armies, nor multinational companies have asked forgiveness. In one way or another the church has.

The plea for forgiveness was certainly ambiguous. Some bishops – those who live with indigenous and black people, who still bear the mark of their oppression today, centuries of suffering and indignity – asked sincerely. Others were less sincere. For example, the cardinal archbishop of Santo Domingo – president of CELAM and the second vice-president of the assembly – did not allow the mass for forgiveness to be celebrated in his cathedral. And we must also remember that, although it was fairly clear for what sins forgiveness was being sought, it was less clear who were the sinners of five centuries ago: whether it was just the conquistadors or also the clerics. So here was no reason for triumphalism. Nevertheless, the fact that John Paul II asked forgiveness in Santo Domingo and did so again when he returned to Rome, the fact that the bishops also did so in a eucharist and introduced it into some parts of the text, is in itself important. In the sinful and hypocritical world of the North, which thinks it has no need to ask anybody for forgiveness, either for the violent deaths it caused in Vietnam, Afghanistan, Iraq, El Salvador, Guatemala, Grenada, Panama, or for the slow death it is inflicting on the south of the planet, asking for forgiveness is a good thing and purifies the air we breathe.

So it is good that forgiveness was sought in Santo Domingo. But in order that this action may evangelise cultures, all of us, clergy, the Pope, bishops, priests, monks and nuns, must perform it with real conviction, not as a sort of quick fix. We must have a firm purpose of amendment and a spirit of reparation towards black and indigenous people. We must ask forgiveness like Bishop Leonidas Proaño on his deathbed: ask the church to make up for all the wrong it has done to the indigenous people. And repentance cannot just stay in the past; the church must have the honesty to ask forgiveness in and for the present, or repentance for the past will have no credibility. Finally, it is necessary that forgiveness should be sought with a real readiness to be forgiven. For, although it may seem paradoxical, this is the most difficult thing, since, in Karl Rahner's famous phrase, 'only those who have been forgiven know they are sinners'. But this is also the most Christian thing, because then forgiveness becomes a gift and an unexpected grace to us from the victims and those we have offended.

The church benefits this world when it humbly and honestly seeks forgiveness and is prepared to receive it as a grace. Thus it can evangelise the culture and cure it of hypocrisy and arrogance. Santo Domingo cautiously opened the way and the church must pursue it and offer it to all.

3. The sin of the world and the sin of the church

In the western world there is an official line according to which, although there are serious problems, the world is going all right or at least better than before. With the fall of the Eastern bloc and many military regimes, with gradual democratisation, even though this is often merely formal, and the imposition – without opposition – of economic neo-liberalism, we have arrived at 'the end of history'. We hear this repeatedly, even though everyday experience – and a technical report by the United Nations – show that at least for the moment, things are getting worse in the world as a whole, and promises that they will soon improve are not credible for the majority, in the wake of countless similar promises.

In this context, following Medellín and Puebla, Santo Domingo did two important things: it was an exercise in fundamental honesty about the real situation and the morality of it. Once again it denounced the terrible situation of poverty and injustice and criticised economic neo-liberalism, not just because it offers an insufficient and barely human attempt at a solution, but because it increases poverty. Many bishops outside the conference hall and the text itself declared this. We are in a bad state and it is getting worse, they said. Some quotations: 'growing impoverishment', 'the statistics show eloquently that during the last decade poverty has increased both in absolute and in relative terms', 'neo-liberal policy makes the negative results even worse'. So, in the tradition of Puebla, 'we must lengthen the list of suffering faces'.

How much notice the world will take of Santo Domingo saying this, I do not know. For this world which applauded John Paul II for his contribution to the fall of the East ignored him when he denounced the war on Iraq. The same could happen now with Santo Domingo, which may well be ignored in this fundamental denunciation of the sin of institutionalised injustice. Nevertheless, the very fact that Santo Domingo insisted on telling the truth is in itself evangelising in a culture of indifference and injustice; it refused to co-operate in the cover-up and institutionalised lie that the world is now on the right track after the disappearance of real socialism.

Secondly, Santo Domingo has once again repeated the option for the poor, a preferential option, based on the Word of God and not on an ideological standpoint, but nevertheless, in John Paul II's words 'a firm and irrevocable' option, which gives 'the measure of our following of Christ'. Utopically and without much technical detail, the bishops offered as an alternative to neo-liberalism an 'economy of solidarity', that is, an economy geared towards a possible life for the masses – and not just as a possible positive spin-off from neo-liberalism, which always directly favours the 'haves'.

The denunciation of unjust poverty and the option for the poor of course evangelise our world. For even the terms 'justice' and 'injustice'

36

are disappearing from this world's official vocabulary – as if they had nothing to do with the world's evils or their solutions, and it was bad-mannered or ignorant to mention them. Moreover, the option for the poor sounds like a macabre euphemism when hardly any countries manage to give even 0.7 per cent of GDP in aid to underdeveloped countries. But triumphalism is also out of place here.

Although some bishops, like Cardinal Arns, for example, personally identified themselves forcefully with these denunciations and exposures, the texts do not have the pathos of the Medellín and Puebla declarations. Perhaps it is lack of freshness, but also because there is no glimpse of that decision to fight for justice and run risks which was present in the previous texts. Strictly speaking, the texts describe the tragedy we are living in, but they are not denunciations of it, they do not unmask it and in no way confront those responsible for the tragedy they describe. Confrontation is very necessary, even though the whole world wants to decrease the level of confrontation. To give a single example, the Atlacatl battalion, which is known to have committed the El Mozote massacre and the murder of the Jesuits in El Salvador, among other things, still brandishes its slogan proclaiming 'For country and with God'. In such a case it is not enough to denounce the reality but we must confront those responsible.

However bold the texts, everyone is aware of the disappearance of the generation of bishops who put these words into practice and engaged in serious confrontation with the public authorities. This seems to be a conscious policy on the part of the Vatican. Not that there are none at all, of course, but governments, armies and oligarchies know very well that there are now fewer and fewer bishops like Sergio Mendes Arceo, Oscar Romero, Leonidas Proaño, Helder Câmara. This means that words about injustice and opting for the poor, although almost identical to the earlier texts, say less today than they did. The US vice-president Nelson Rockefeller reacted immediately against Medellín, and Ronald Reagan's advisers against Puebla. To date we do not find the powers of this world have felt threatened or even affected by Santo Domingo. They have not condemned it and possibly, now that the East has fallen, they have lost interest in criticism from religious bodies.

We should like also to add that if denouncing the sin of injustice and opting for the poor is evangelising culture, we fail to evangelise if we ignore the sin within the church itself, and its contribution to the sin of the world, through action and above all omission. This is a very old problem, I know, but we must emphasise it again. For the majority of bishops at Santo Domingo, to say nothing of the Vatican, it seems that the world's evils – injustice, dictatorships, corruption, scams – are always the work of 'others', communists, military dictators, even capitalists (as in the past it was rationalists, protestants, unbelievers and pagans...) and that all these evils would have been avoided if people had paid heed to the church. This is not only baseless triumphalism; it fails to preach the gospel. The church loses credibility if it only denounces what is wrong outside and does not sincerely and humbly recognise what is wrong within.

This recognition of its own sin did not occur even minimally at Santo Domingo. The church is much readier to see the sin outside than inside. When it looks to itself, it notes the sins, weaknesses or dangers in lay men and women rather than in priests, in monks and nuns rather than in the hierarchy, who appear to be immune, on principle, from every human weakness.

I am not of course advocating an impossible perfection or a paralysing masochism, but we must be aware that here once again is a lost opportunity to evangelise culture. In a hypocritical world which does not want to ask forgiveness for the oppression it inflicts on two-thirds of the planet, which even passes off as historical greatness what is often depredation and destruction of other peoples, it would be Christian –more so than any words – for the church simply to recognise its own limitations and sins.

4. Recognition of the 'other'

Santo Domingo's greatest theoretical contribution is to have approached and recognised the 'other' – the right to difference – more clearly than in previous church documents; in particular to have recognised women, indigenous and blacks. For however difficult it is to recognise the 'poor', it is even more difficult to recognise the 'other', even though frequently both coincide in the same person or group. Of course the 'poor' make a tremendous ethical and theological demand, but the 'other' reaches to the very roots not only of the liturgy, but also the mediation of the faith, dogma, theology and teaching of the church and so on. The 'other' really introduces us not only to what is different, but to the unknown.

The bishops concentrated on the 'other' for a variety of reasons. Out of shame and responsibility, something serious had to be said about indigenous and blacks on the fifth centenary. Some bishops said they could not go back to their diocese without a serious text on these matters. As for the matter of women, it is also evident that we cannot continue as we have done up till now and the church cannot detach itself from these matters or trivialise the problems by simplistic treatment. In fact the most vigorous texts were on these subjects, though perhaps this was due to their novelty within the church.

Time will show what effect these texts have. It will depend on whether bishops and pastoral workers really become involved in these 'other' cultures, if they are open to them, give to them and receive from them, if the Vatican encourages all this or at least does not hinder it. In short, if the church overcomes its age-old habits of colonialism, paternalism, machismo and clericalism and works against them.

As well as overcoming habits, the church must also learn. This is by no means easy because it must learn about things it thinks it already knows about. At present the possible ordination of women is causing great consternation, even though there does not appear to be any insuperable dogmatic difficulty. It is presented for the moment as a problem without solution. So what can we say about a liturgy, ethics, dogmatics based on the 'other'? That is, based on the really unknown, on what is by definition not manageable through ingrained ideas and practices.

For the 'other' is an effective mediation of what there is of 'otherness' in God's own mystery. Standing before the other, letting it be other, is an effective way of standing before God's mystery. It was not easy in the past, nor is it easy today. Nevertheless, this, and not just liturgical romanticism, as Bishop Pedro Casaldáliga says, is what is required in accepting the reality of women, indigenous people, blacks, mestizos, the 'other'.

So here are important, but difficult, advances. From the point of view of evangelising culture, with respect to women's recognition, it must be said that the world has evangelised the church before the church evangelised the world. So here the church must learn from the world and be grateful. With respect to the indigenous and blacks, if the church really accepts, values and welcomes them, it will be evangelising a culture which still today – in spite of universal democratic declarations of equality

– ignores, oppresses and despises the other, tries to keep difference geographically and anthropologically distant; a culture in which, recently, in various countries in the North of the planet, we have seen serious and alarming outbreaks of xenophobia.

So it is good that Santo Domingo should have spoken about the 'other', but it is necessary for the church to defend this 'other' in its pastoral work and run the necessary risks to do so.

5. Theology in retreat

In theology, there has been a retreat. Fundamentally, theology has retreated in its procedure, its method. The events of history are no longer seen as a sign of the times in a strictly theological sense, that is, as the place where God can speak his word and in which he himself can be present, as God. This is a serious backward step, both from Vatican II, which declared the reality and importance of the signs of the times for the church's mission, and from Medellín and Puebla, which scrutinised them in action and based their theological thinking on them.

As I have mentioned, in Santo Domingo the presidency imposed the sequence judge-see-act, which means first do your theology, then see what the world is like and lastly apply your theology to the world. This means 'judging' from 'God's' viewpoint something you have not yet 'seen'. And trying to see God in quoted biblical texts from the past without having seen God in the reality of the present.

Of course the relation between seeing and judging, between reality and theology, is dialectical. So we should not think that, just from seeing, a correct judgment will mechanically follow, that theology will mechanically arise from experience alone. But within the necessary hermeneutical circle, we have to maintain what is fundamental for all Christian theology, based on a God who has become history: there can be no theology without previous historical reality, we cannot meet God in texts from the past without listening to his reality in the present.

This point expressed here in the abstract has serious repercussions in the Santo Domingo theology. One of these is that its christology, proclaimed as the connecting backbone of the whole document, is not based on Jesus of Nazareth, but on an abstract Christ, in accordance with the logic described above. Jesus is judged as Christ without having first seen the reality of that Christ who is Jesus. Thus the historical Jesus disappears, the one who was present at Medellín, in *Evangelii Nuntiandi* and at Puebla, perhaps more in the form of energy than in particular texts. He is certainly present in the more committed communities and where there have been the most martyrs, and of course present in liberation theology. Nevertheless, at Santo Domingo a choice was made to begin by proclaiming the Christ of faith rather than by looking at Jesus of Nazareth.

Another consequence of this procedure is that – ironically – the best texts are not the theological ones, in which the bishops should be experts, but the historical. In fact the more strictly theological texts which begin each chapter are notoriously vague and lacking in inspiration. Of course they cite passages from scripture, councils and popes, but although these possess the authority of the magisterium and some of them are inspired, they are not inspiring.

To put it most radically, 'God loved us' is a central text which expresses an essential and consoling truth of faith. But if this text is not set in the context of a particular situation, it can sound merely spiritualistic, and therefore routine, without power to mobilise the energies of the spirit. On the other hand, if it is seen as the culmination of an account of the victims of this world, with their martyred love and hope, then this same text can express God's solidarity and tenderness towards them, so that the text becomes good news.

The theological procedure I have described is something that directly concerns only the church and, at most, intellectuals. Nevertheless, I think it also has evangelising potential in the environment we move in, because in our world people frequently proceed from ideological preconceptions, which are not tested against reality. Often something which 'is right' and 'is the solution' has been decided on in advance, whatever may be happening in the world. Thus some say 'democracy' is right. So are 'neo-liberalism', 'the need for armies', or 'modernism' or 'postmodernism' (although the latter, by definition, cannot proclaim itself to be absolute truth).

If we seek a parallel between this phenomenon and the church's faith, it will no doubt be argued that there is no comparison between the truth of ideologies or human institutions and the truth of faith. It will be said that faith contains the truth independently of what happens in the world. But without entering into a theoretical discussion about this here, we can reply that pastorally at least, it is very important that what we might call the generic truth of faith becomes truth in the real world, that is, active and relevant truth, and this happens when it stands in contrast to actual situations.

The pastoral relevance of faith depends on its capacity to be illuminated (verified and 'truthed', if I may use the word) by the events of history. If this is said of faith, even more so should it be said of theology. My point here is that a way of living and understanding faith and theology, open to life, tested by life, and enriched by life – beginning, even if only logically, with 'seeing' life – is a way of evangelising culture, overcoming preconceptions and dogma, so clearly perceived now in the questioned methods of Christendom and in the failed dogmatic versions of Marxism; it is also equally necessary if we are to overcome neo-liberalism, modernism, pragmatism, post-modernism, when they tend to become dogmatic systems.

One thing the world needs today is to 'see' life without manipulating it, even more so to 'listen to it'. For, as Karl Rahner said, 'Reality wants to take the floor.' With Medellín and Puebla, the message of real life becomes a piercing cry. Let us hope the church of Jesus can help the world in this difficult task. And certainly if liberation theology, though silenced and even vilified, has produced good in our world, this has happened as a result of its honesty in looking at the real world, listening to the people's cries and trying to answer them.

6. The silence about the martyrs

The most shocking result of not beginning by 'seeing' reality was the silence about the martyrs. Of course in prayer meetings the bishops remembered Archbishop Romero and other Latin American martyrs, but this does not make up for the incredible silence in the text. This silence is not broken by the addition of a line at the end of the chapter recalling the 500 years of evangelisation which recognises 'those who have even borne witness by shedding their blood for the love of Jesus'. The text's extreme brevity, its ambiguous historical context – does it include the martyrs of today? – and its complete lack of historical and theological analysis, which are in fact so vital, make it look more like a tacked-on phrase to get out of a tight corner, rather than having any deep conviction about the centrality of martyrdom.

Whatever the explanation – danger that their words might be manipulated, caution imposed by canon law, conflicts it might lead the church into – certainly no one in countries like El Salvador and Guatemala understands why the martyrs are not only not greatly valued but not even mentioned. For in Latin America martyrdom is not an incident or an exception, but a massive reality which cannot be hidden. It is the novelty, the grace, the credential and seal of the most genuine evangelisation that has taken place between Medellín and Santo Domingo. Therefore this silence is absolutely incomprehensible, highly suspect and above all, greatly impoverishing.

Ignoring the martyrs means really refusing to consider the signs of the times, both as these describe what characterises the epoch – martyrdom in huge numbers is the newest and most characteristic sign in recent Latin American church history – and as they express, by their special quality, the presence of God among us. It also means depriving ourselves of an irreplaceable hermeneutic principle for understanding Jesus, since the martyrs of today, unlike the martyrs throughout history, die as Jesus died, for the same cause as Jesus, because – structurally – they lived like Jesus. It also shows an ignorance of the historical and theological origin of the church itself, which was really born after the martyrdom of Jesus, to continue Jesus' life and in the hope of resurrection, that is, that God did justice to Jesus the martyr. It means failing to take advantage of the principle source of credibility for the church today, which is so important for announcing God's mystery to unbelievers, and to strengthen the faith of doubters, so vital for telling the poor that God loves them. Finally it shows ingratitude to the martyrs themselves, depriving their families of consolation, failing to recognise those who continue to be a light and encouragement for the communities... As we saw in the long text we quoted above, the *Secunda Relatio* proceeds in exactly the opposite manner. Thus certain points become clear: there was strong tension with the Vatican and there are divisions in the Latin American church, for not a single echo of this splendid text has remained in the final document. It also shows that there are groups of bishops, and many committees behind them, for whom the martyrs, set in the violent current context of their countries, are witnesses to faith and love, essential and irreplaceable witnesses for those who are trying to live by faith and love today.

This text I quoted, which is both obvious and surprising, recalls the martyrs and puts them at the centre. It develops an important theology about why there is martyrdom and why these martyrs are central. This text and, of course, the reality behind it – the fact of martyrdom for the sake of love and the grateful recognition given to this by Christians – is good news, is gospel for the poor of this world. At the same time it frightens the powerful – in El Salvador they are still afraid of Archbishop Romero and Father Ellacuría – as is predicted in John's gospel. Nevertheless, those who killed Archbishop Romero and the Atlacatl battalion that murdered the Jesuits, the two women and many others, use and abuse God's name and still call themselves Catholics.

There can be endless theoretical discussion about what the 'new' evangelisation consists of. But the answer must contain one essential obvious ingredient: that it recaptures – in a new way, possibly – the good news Jesus of Nazareth brought and was in his own life. It is above all the martyrs who do this. They are the ones in our day who proclaim God's kingdom to the poor, who tell them that life, fellowship and dignity are possible, who confront the idols that make the poor become victims and who tell the poor that God loves them. And they are the ones who recreate in our day the gospel preached by Paul: Jesus the martyr crucified and risen. Therefore, once more, it is simply incredible that Santo Domingo should not mention the martyrs, the best thing the Latin American church has produced, the best we have.

Moreover, by not mentioning them, it fails to evangelise culture, it fails to purify with the martyrs' honesty, compassion and love the corrupt atmosphere of lies, indifference and oppression in our world. In that world, neither armies, nor governments nor oligarchies keep martyrs alive. Neither do many political parties, universities or the media. So our culture becomes de-christianised, dehumanised. Making it become human and Christian is not just a matter of words, but it also involves imbuing it with honesty, compassion and the real love shown by the martyrs.

III. PRINCIPLES FOR MAKING THE SANTO DOMINGO EVENT PRODUCTIVE

As we have just seen, many and various winds blew at Santo Domingo, some better and some worse. Positively and negatively, Santo Domingo as a whole is a faithful reflection of the situation of the universal church and the Latin American church. In the universal church there is a sustained movement of reaction which starts from the centre and receives reasonable support on the periphery, from some persons of good will according to their conscience and others more ideological. In the Latin American church there is still a serious struggle to maintain or defeat the spirit of Medellín.

Taken as a whole, Santo Domingo is certainly not a reason for rejoicing. This can be noted even in the bishops' reactions. But neither should it be a reason for paralysing discouragement, because evangelical and Latin American winds also blew there — even though they hardly ever prevailed as they should have done. In our opinion the most negative thing about Santo Domingo is the sadness of a lost opportunity to go deeper into the tasks facing the church, and above all to be much more sensitive to the cries emerging from the Latin American situation and evangelise culture more strongly.

Nevertheless, Santo Domingo must be made productive, because the event provides a basis for this, and because the poor of the Latin American continent expect this and need it. So we must seek illuminating and encouraging principles. I think these have to be looked for outside rather than within the conference. This is also why I speak of principles for making Santo Domingo productive rather than intrinsic principles for interpreting Santo Domingo itself.

The latter is really difficult because the differences and tensions were so great that I do not think it possible to find anything that sufficiently unites the event and the text. Of course there were also divisions and tensions at Puebla but 'the preferential option for the poor' very quickly became in practice the interpretive principle of the whole text — and also had in its favour the possibility of becoming so in principle. But there was nothing like that at Santo Domingo. No single theme imposed itself as a unifying principle of the whole conference. And if it is said that christology was such a principle — as in a way the Vatican pretended —its presentation was so abstract that it could not perform this function.

So, if not within the event itself, we must search outside it for principles that, although they cannot unify such a diverse event, will nevertheless allow the best things in the event and the text to become productive. I think these principles are as follows:

1. To make Santo Domingo really productive we have to take seriously what was stated there: that this conference should be considered as a continuity from Medellín and Puebla. This does not mean primarily that the texts should be compared or that a synopsis should be made of the three conferences, although of course this would be very useful. What it means, in my opinion, is recognising that the Latin American church should still continue in the spirit of Medellín, and this not just as an arbitrary decision but because there is still none better. Of course, this does not mean that there are no new agendas for the church. But it does mean that it is very dangerous to insist on the need for a new approach when by and large this has been the reality of the church since Medellín.

In particular, when Santo Domingo calls for the evangelisation of cultures – and let's hope the church will pursue it – and of the need to take on indigenous and black culture as a challenge to the church, we should not forget that Medellín already proclaimed this fundamental necessity when it demanded that the church should become incarnate in historical reality. Not that these two things are exactly the same, but neither are they separate. And what Medellín still teaches today is a real movement towards becoming incarnate among the poor as the fundamental means of evangelising Latin American culture, on the one hand, and for the church to take on their culture, on the other.

The same could be said about the 'new evangelisation'. This already began at Medellín, where, indeed, the expression was forged before it became popularised by John Paul II. The new approach sought now pales in comparison with the new step taken then. Now what is being asked is that evangelisation should be new in its expression, methods and fervour, but curiously, there is no new thinking about what evangelisation actually is. And this is precisely what did happen at Medellín. It did not so much discuss the novelty of the things surrounding and accompanying evangelisation, but simply and centrally what it means to preach the gospel. In addition Puebla also took a decisive step forward, which has not been surpassed in the new evangelisation of today, in saying that there was not only a need to evangelise but also to be evangelised –gratefully, humbly and joyfully – by the poor.

2. Although here I have concentrated more on the event of Santo Domingo than the texts, let me now say a word about the texts and about how they can be made productive. In general, many observers, including many bishops, have recognised that a good number of the texts are very weak, especially those in the first half of the document. Other texts, as we have seen, are better, especially because of the new ideas they introduce.

In my opinion, in order to make them productive, we have to select. This has nothing to do with manipulation but is mere common sense. Moreover, history itself will select them, as happened at Medellín and Puebla, in a way that will not be arbitrary or dependent on propaganda campaigns and manipulation. But as well as selecting the texts most useful to communities, we must set them in their real context. They must be evaluated and related to the actual tasks they promote and demand. This work must be supported institutionally, that is, by the bishops who approved the texts.

If the most novel texts really become productive, then, as some have said, Santo Domingo could even represent an advance for the Latin American church. But we must understand this in the right way. Of course Santo Domingo represents an advance in the church's agenda, which can no longer ignore the issues of women, indigenous and black people, ecology. And this new agenda is reflected in some of the texts. But in order to speak of a real advance, we must add a particular church context to the text, that is, the decision to support it, to make it productive, and to defend it when society – as is bound to happen if the church really decides to defend indigenous and black people – reacts and persecutes.

3. Finally, if I ask what was really at stake at Santo Domingo, what caused discussions, tensions and Vatican interventions, and what, therefore, in my opinion, can function as a guiding principle for the future, I believe it is the Latin American church's identity. Fundamentally Santo Domingo was – and continues to be – a struggle about what it means to be a church, a Christian, a believer in Latin America.

The real issue at Santo Domingo was the new identity of the Latin American church. The problem can be concealed in various ways, by alluding to problems of communion with Rome, dangers or exaggerations in orthodoxy and liturgy, liberation theology and so on. But the truth is that neither bishops nor theologians nor base communities have serious problems about communion with the church or loyal obedience. What is happening is something else, the new thing that has happened in the church since Medellín, and which can be summed up in the following three points.

Firstly, for the first time in centuries, the Latin American church has become itself. In this historical process over the last 30 years, the church has become both Latin American and Christian. The real situation of Latin America has led us to a better understanding and practice of the gospel. This in turn has led us to a better understanding of and action upon historical reality. The fact that, for the first time, being a Christian and being a Latin American are not contradictory in any way but a mutual enrichment is the greatest novelty of our time. This has been the result of much creativity and also much conflict. Some bishops in Latin America and in the Vatican were frightened by this. The first thing at issue, therefore, has been the Latin Americanisation of the church and the struggle to maintain or diminish it.

The second point, which is connected with the first, is that for the first time in centuries the Latin American church has been socially relevant in accordance with the gospel. It has not basically preached itself and defended itself as an institution, or sought to defend its ancient privileges. Rather, like Jesus, it has looked at the world of sin and tried to transform it into the utopia of God's kingdom. This was also what was at issue at Santo Domingo: whether the church should look at itself or at this world of sin and hope. That is why I accorded such importance to the analysis of martyrdom in the Latin American church. Our analysis was present in the *Secunda Relatio* and absent from Santo Domingo. Martyrdom is the most convincing proof of taking the real world seriously, taking on its sin in order to bring the crucified down from the cross.

The third point is that evangelisation was of course still directed at members of the church but also – and this was a new departure – at the world. This was not an effort to 'Christianise' it superficially, but to humanise it, by introducing more human values, which are also the most divine and those expressed by Jesus in his own life: honesty, freedom, fellowship, welcoming those who are different. This is how the church is bringing about God's kingdom, through evangelising culture, the reality in which we live. But this means that the church must be, and often has been, a society that stands in contrast, introducing truth, humility, compassion into the world and against a world of lies, arrogance, indifference, cruelty.

In this essay I have used the metaphor of wind. Following this metaphor we may conclude by saying that Santo Domingo was certainly not a gale like the 'violent wind' of Pentecost. In general, we are living in a church whose windows, opened by the Vatican Council, are now closing again, and whose air has grown stale once more. But at Santo Domingo, and above all in the daily reality of the Latin American churches, the breeze of Medellín, symbolised in the *Secunda Relatio*, is still blowing. And at times of commitment and hope, especially times of martyrdom, this breeze becomes a gale and, whatever happens, come wind come wrack, many continue to go forward.

So it is not a routine conclusion or merely making a virtue of necessity to say that it is up to the Latin American church to make the best of the Santo Domingo event and its texts productive. For, as I have tried to show, many winds blew there and some were favourable. If, with such powers against them — political, economic, cultural, military, religious and sometimes even within the church — there are Christians who continue their journey guided by the Church's new identity, the spirit of Medellín, this means that the Spirit of Jesus and the Spirit of God are still at work. And in this Spirit we can continue to advance.

Translated by Dinah Livingstone

This essay was first published in *Revista Latinoamericana de Teología*, No. 27, 1992, pp.273-93.

An Agenda

GUSTAVO GUTIÉRREZ

Many things paved the way for the final document of the fourth Latin American Bishops' Conference in Santo Domingo. Among them were long preparation, many expectations, quite a few tensions and fears in various quarters, together with some long-established mistrust, the powerful presence of an agenda for the church, new moves at the last minute, the serenity and pastoral sense of many participants, the growing poverty of the Latin American people and many people's prayers.

The days of the conference itself were also busy and complicated. A rather confused working method and other factors made it impossible to produce a document with a theological scope comparable to that of previous Bishops' Conferences. But this had not been the intention. At various points the Santo Domingo text simply refers to these conferences for its doctrinal framework and basic options.

These are therefore crucial to its interpretation.[1] In this respect the Santo Domingo text (henceforth abbreviated to SD) makes important clarifications and sets out, invitingly rather than with threats of anathema, points on the agenda put forward by Latin American Christians in recent years.

There will be plenty of reports on the stages of the preparatory process and plenty of observers to describe the vicissitudes and tensions experienced during the bishops' assembly. All this is important for understanding the document. This article will emphasise the core of the document, the tasks that lie ahead. The challenges are enormous and require all our energy.

50

I. ONE OPTION AND THREE PASTORAL DIRECTIONS

From the initial preparation onwards there was present at Santo Domingo the perspective of new evangelisation, proclaimed at Medellín and vigorously reasserted recently by John Paul II.

The first documents in the preliminary stage to Santo Domingo presented and juxtaposed two great challenges for preaching the gospel in Latin America. On the one hand it was stated that the most important came from modern culture, the 'incoming culture', in the expression used at Puebla.[2] But on the other hand it was stated that the greatest challenge came from the enormous poverty existing in Latin America. It was even stated that 'the presupposition of the new evangelisation is the preferential option for the poor in solidarity'.

As the theme developed, the relationship between the modern world and poverty became clearer. It also became clear that the various challenges to the work of preaching the gospel had to be tackled as a whole. The task had to be approached from the starting point of the abject poverty of the marginalised majority of the Latin American people. The debate was driven by commentaries and criticism of the preparatory documents and in particular by the contributions from the continent's individual episcopates.[3]

These contributions were collected in the text called the *Secunda Relatio*, which was of crucial importance in the lead-up to Santo Domingo. It became the basis for the 'Working Document' (henceforth WD) which provided an adequate basis for the work of the conference and could have been very useful in the composition of its texts. Nevertheless, on one crucial point the Final Document clarifies and refines certain terms used by the WD which could have led to confusion. I refer to the list of options for the Latin American church offered by the WD under the heading 'preferential options' (WD, paras 620-41).[4] Among these, as well as the option for the poor, we find the option for the young (already mentioned by Puebla), the family, the laity, evangelisation of modern culture and others. Santo Domingo does not follow this list but rightly distinguishes between the preferential option for the poor and priorities in pastoral work.[5]

This is not just a disagreement about words, or an attempt to devalue other pastoral challenges arising out of our situation. Not everyone saw this at the beginning but the point here was the need to keep clearly in sight the gospel perspective that has inspired the pastoral activity of the Latin American church for the last 25 years, with worldwide repercussions. This clarity is required not just for our intellectual satisfaction but for pastoral reasons. The pastoral guidelines offer much more scope when they are linked to the core option.

Thus Santo Domingo strongly reasserts the preferential option for the poor. The theme chosen for the conference was 'Jesus Christ yesterday, today and forever' (Heb 13:8),[6] giving it a christological perspective. So the basis of this option was seen as Christ and his proclamation of the good news to the poor (cf. Lk 4:18-19). 'This,' says Santo Domingo, 'is the fundamental premise which commits us to a preferential option for the poor, in accordance with the gospel, an option which is firm and irrevocable, but not exclusive or excluding, and which was solemnly proclaimed at the Medellín and Puebla conferences' (178, cf. also Message 17). The continuity is clearly maintained and Medellín and Puebla also took care to base the option for the poor on Jesus' witness.

In the following sections (179 and 180) and in many others (cf. 50, 275, 296, 302), it is emphasised that this option is central and therefore at the heart of the various tasks of the church. When one thinks of the resistance aroused in some quarters, inside and outside the church, by this viewpoint, its formulation and even the terms used (the word 'option', for example), it is impossible not to feel that this is a definitive gain.

This is a viewpoint which is both old and new. It was mentioned prophetically by John XXIII on the eve of the Second Vatican Council. It has developed in the recent years of historical commitment and Christian communities' direct contact with the Bible. It has also influenced theological thinking about these developments. It burst on the scene at Medellín, was formulated more precisely in the years that followed, and found its mature expression at Puebla. With John Paul II, the preferential option for the poor has firmly entered the ordinary universal teaching of the church.[7]

It was only recently that Latin American Christians gradually discovered the biblical meaning of commitment to the poor and their liberation. Their discovery was quickly taken up by the church's regional magisterium and has gained great influence in the life of the church and the continent as a whole. This approach has opened up new spaces for the gospel, it has inspired many pastoral initiatives and stimulated theological thinking to follow new paths. It has been sealed by the witness of martyrs and the unassuming daily commitment of so many,[8] and has enabled others to bear suffering of an intensity known to the Lord alone. It has also aroused hopes which have increased deep fidelity to Jesus and his church. This is beyond doubt the most important contribution the Latin American church has made to the universal church, to which it belongs.

By making the preferential option for the poor the basis for the church's activity, Santo Domingo confirms it as a true insight and a valid experience. But we must be careful not to be satisfied with statements and texts. These are important, as the documents of Medellín and Puebla prove, if they become incarnate in the life of the church. There is always a danger that such statements, however important and interesting, may remain just words or playing to the gallery.

This outlook must be translated into specific pastoral guidelines. Santo Domingo formulates these in relation to the main themes chosen for the conference: new evangelisation, human development and inculturated evangelisation. Under the first heading it emphasises the role of the laity (especially the young) in the task of evangelisation and celebrating the faith. It also significantly stresses the missionary role the Latin American church must take on beyond our continent. I am convinced that this is one of the most useful paths we can follow. Puebla has already called upon us to 'give of our poverty' (368). I hope this will indeed be a pastoral direction in the future (cf. 293-95; see also 12 and 57 on the missionary dimension).

The second main pastoral guideline is related to human development. Here stress is laid on heeding the cry of the poor and the need to assume 'with renewed fervour the preferential option for the poor in accordance with the gospel'. This should illuminate 'all our evangelising work in imitation of Jesus Christ'. Likewise it states that 'all human life is sacred', which should inspire us to defend life and the family (cf. 296-97).[9]

The third point is the need for preaching the gospel within the particular culture: 'inculturated evangelisation'. Certainly one of the most salient points in Santo Domingo is the 'inculturation' of the gospel. This is a new term but an old idea and its resonance is incarnation. But the fact is – and the first preaching of the gospel in Latin America proves it all too clearly – the church finds it hard to step outside the world of western culture in preaching the gospel. So Santo Domingo calls for 'a pastoral conversion of the Church' (30; cf. also 23). There is much to be done here, and the fundamental step is to recognise the values held by the indigenous peoples and the black population. We must also accept the challenge of the increasingly rapid urbanisation of the continent and the aggressive presence of the mass media (cf. 298-301).

II. THE NEW FACES OF POVERTY

Santo Domingo recognises the overwhelming fact, clear for all to see, of the growing impoverishment of the Latin American masses. The cry of the poor, mentioned by Medellín, which Puebla calls 'clear, growing, impetuous and at times threatening' (89), has today become deafening. Santo Domingo states that the poverty to which 'millions of our brothers and sisters are subjected, to the point where they suffer extremes of destitution, is the most devastating and humiliating scourge affecting Latin America and the Caribbean' (179).[10] This is one more reason for a preferential option for the poor.

In view of all this, the text invites us to 'lengthen the list of suffering faces' (179) described by Puebla (31-9) in a beautiful passage written by two Latin American bishops who are no longer with us today: Germán Schmitz and Leonidas Proaño. In these faces we must discover the Lord's features;[11] they challenge us to 'profound personal conversion and conversion of the church' (178). They are faces 'disfigured by hunger caused by inflation, foreign debt and social injustices' (ibid.).[12]

Throughout the document particular social sectors illustrate the actual faces of the poor in Latin America. The date of the conference made it obligatory to speak of the continent's indigenous peoples and the black population (whom SD prefers to call African-Americans). They have been marginalised and ill-treated for centuries but on this occasion their values were recognised and their contribution to Latin American history appreciated.

As is well known, it was not easy to find the necessary consensus for the conference – as it had been requested to do for some while – to ask forgiveness of the indigenous and black peoples for the Christian involvement in the oppression and injustice they suffered from the 16th century onwards. SD does ask forgiveness (cf. 20 and 246), but possibly without the clear intervention of the Pope this would not have happened. Various voices objected to the recognition of facts whose historical truth cannot be denied.[13] Fortunately these obstacles were overcome, but much remains to be done in terms of solidarity with indigenous and black peoples and cultures of Latin America. This is a crucial element of the agenda before us. The poor not only have their own culture and often their own language. The condition of women – especially poor women – is also a feature of this situation. In a celebrated text Puebla speaks of women as 'doubly oppressed and marginalised' (1134 note) and devotes several paragraphs to an analysis of their situation (cf. 834-49). SD also devotes a section to this theme (104-110). Here abuses against on women are denounced and also the persistent mentality (in both society and church) which marginalises them. This is an important contribution but it would have been interesting to see more about women's organisations 'demanding respect for their rights', which Puebla mentioned (836). There is no doubt that women are one of the most dynamic and creative groups both in society and in the church in Latin America. The document is right to say it is necessary to 'go more deeply into the role of women' in both (105). Let us hope this will be done.[14]

III. SIGNS OF THE TIMES

In recent years the Christian communities of Latin America and accompanying theological reflection have developed an interest in new issues or taken older ones in new directions. These themes come out of the historical context and have shown themselves to be true signs of the times which have to be appreciated in the preaching of the Gospel, and their call to commitment must be heeded.

Santo Domingo notes some of these phenomena which are opening up new spaces for historical solidarity, in particular with the poorest, and for the understanding of the faith. The attention we pay them should help us overcome the divorce between faith and life to which Santo Domingo refers on numerous occasions (cf. 24,44,48). Santo Domingo lists some of these 'new signs of the times in the field of human development', but we also find them in other sections of the document. And throughout we find the forceful reiteration of the centrality of the preferential option for the poor. Let us look at a few examples from this list.

One of the gravest problems in Latin America in recent decades has been – and still is – the violation of human rights. Many Christians and some churches as institutions have made a special – and risky – commitment to this field. The subject was discussed at Puebla (cf. the document 'Human Dignity') but Santo Domingo is more detailed. Even though at times this reflects the fear some felt that this subject could be manipulated (cf. 168), Santo Domingo also makes quite clear that human rights are violated by the poverty and injustice that exist in Latin America (cf. 167).

One of humanity's main concerns today is ecology. Understandably, this concern arose first in the rich industrialised countries. Nevertheless, it would be wrong to think that it is an artificial concern in poor countries. So Santo Domingo offers a reading of the problem from the standpoint of 'the world's poor masses' (168). In fact they are often victims of the rich countries' development. So Santo Domingo calls for 'an ecological ethic', which 'demands the abandonment of utilitarian individualistic morality' (ibid.). And here it reminds us of a subject which I think will be very important in future, 'the universal destination of the goods of creation' (ibid.).

In this connection, it also reminds us of the importance of land as a gift of creation. Of course it is of particular importance to peasants, many of whom belong to indigenous peoples. They have a religious vision of 'mother earth', which provides their sustenance. This is opposed to the 'commercial view which considers the earth only in terms of exploitation and profit' and even worse, 'reaching the point of uprooting and expelling its legitimate owners' (172). The latter is a process which began five centuries ago and which is still going on. Rural poverty has clearly identifiable causes.

Painfully, after a long period involving great suffering, Latin American countries are moving towards democratic governments. Only in these conditions is it possible to begin the process of building just and pluralistic societies. In some countries the church played an important part in the democratisation process (cf. 190).[15] Realistically, however, Santo Domingo recognises that in practice democracy is 'still more formal than real' (191). It also points out that democracy will only take root if the people who have secured it have a leading role in it in Latin America (cf. 191 and 193).

A necessary condition for genuine respect for human rights and a democratic organisation of society is the establishment of social justice. Santo Domingo deals directly with what today is one of the most controversial issues in Latin America, economic neo-liberalism. This is one of the best sections of the Santo Domingo document. In the face of 'the impoverishment and widening gap between rich and poor' (199), it calls for 'the establishment of an economics based on real and effective solidarity' (201). This should control 'those mechanisms of the market economy which do fundamental harm to the poor' (202). Following in the footsteps of John Paul II, Santo Domingo also denounces the mortgaging of our countries' development by foreign debt and asserts that this debt cannot be paid at the expense of the lives of the poorest (cf. 197).

Although it is not considered to be one of the signs of the times, it is important to note the challenge (among many others, of course) represented by the process of urbanisation taking place in Latin America. The subject was touched on at Medellín and discussed at Puebla. Santo Domingo returns to it and shows that it involves a profound cultural change. It also notes that the poverty and misery of most urban dwellers is increasing 'as a result of exploitative and excluding economic models' (255).

We have noted some of the challenges confronting the proclamation of 'the Gospel of justice, love and mercy' (13).[16] They are all connected with the situation of the poor, the vast majority of the continent, and they call for solidarity with those who suffer marginalisation and injustice. 'All evangelisation must be... an inculturation of the Gospel,' says Santo Domingo in its profession of faith (13). This process embraces not only the ancient cultures of the continent but must also take into account the challenges already mentioned. The Gospel must also be inculturated in them. This effort is 'imperative for the following of Jesus and necessary to repair the disfigured face of the world' (13). This means its object 'will always be the whole salvation and liberation of a particular people or human group (243).[17] Salvation and liberation are the opposite of the relentless force of the structures of sin manifest in modern society' (ibid.).[18]

Within the doctrinal and pastoral framework of Medellín and Puebla, though without the prophetic sweep of the former or the theological density of the latter, Santo Domingo takes up a number of points on the agenda which Latin American Christians have begun to establish in recent years. It clearly sets out the new challenges. How well they are met will depend – as with previous Latin American Bishops' Conferences – on the reception we are able to give to the Santo Domingo texts. If we listen to their call we will leave behind debilitating internal squabbles and go forward in solidarity with all who live on this continent, especially the poor and oppressed, and grow in the communion of the church. In this way we shall welcome the free gift of the Kingdom in the Latin American people's history of suffering and hope.

Notes

1   There are very few explicit quotations of Medellín and Puebla texts, but there are numerous references to the message of these conferences, and Santo Domingo clearly states its continuity with them.

2   The expression is used only once in the Santo Domingo text (cf. 30).

3   These have been published by CELAM: *Aportes de las Conferencias Episcopales a la IV Conferencia* (Bogotá 1992).

4   Though in the body of the text only the option for the poor is called 'preferential'; the others are simply called 'options'.

5   Cf. the observations on this point in various articles published in *Páginas* 117 (September 1992) devoted to the Santo Domingo Conference.

6   Cf. the important work by C.I. González, *Jesucristo ayer, hoy y siempre* (CELAM, Bogotá 1991) and M. Díaz Mateos, 'Jesucristo ayer, hoy y siempre' in *Páginas* (September 1992), pp.58-71.

7   But everyone was aware that its repetition by the Pope, in particular in his opening speech at the Santo Domingo Conference, was one of the reasons for its presence in the Santo Domingo text. 'In continuity with the Conferences of Medellín and Puebla,' John Paul II says significantly, 'the church reaffirms the preferential option for the poor' (16).

8   I regret the Santo Domingo text was not clearer on this painful but also hopeful wealth in the Latin American church: its martyrs.

9   I shall return later to some points raised in the chapter on human development.

10   The fact that the conference was held on a Caribbean island encouraged greater exactitude of expression: the text always speaks of Latin America and the Caribbean.

11   The Santo Domingo text refers explicitly to Mt 25:31-46, a tacit reference in the Puebla text.

12   There follows a list of examples of these faces.

13   In the Pope's message of 13 October addressed to Afro-Americans there is a clear recognition of the injustice suffered by 'the black populations of the African continent' and a request for forgiveness for the Christian share in this ill-treatment. John Paul II had already asked forgiveness on the Island of Gorée (Senegal) in February 1992. The members of the conference appeared less convinced about asking the indigenous peoples for forgiveness. In this case, given the enormity of what happened, the questioning of colonialism that asking forgiveness implies and the emotions it arouses, things were more controversial. But on 21 October in Rome the Pope spoke of his journey to Santo Domingo as an 'expiation' for the sin, injustice and violence committed by Christians when they arrived in these lands. This led him to a 'prayer for forgiveness' addressed, especially, to the first inhabitants of the new continent, *the Indians* and also to those who were taken there from Africa as slaves to do

gruelling work' (our italics). Confronted with this, even the most recalcitrant had to give in.

14 The preparatory text on women contained important elements which did not reach the Santo Domingo conclusions.

15 The text proves this in the appropriate place, theoretically, in the light of theology. In spite of its brief, in the Santo Domingo text we often find that real situations are in fact described at the beginning of the subjects treated. It is difficult to go against a traditional – and logical – approach.

16 The text approved at Santo Domingo only said 'Gospel of justice'. The addition is one of the few modifications resulting from its revision in Rome.

17 The notion of integral or total liberation has been present in Latin American theology since Medellín and Puebla, which distinguish three levels or planes: liberation from unjust structures, liberation of the human person and liberation from sin. The latter is considered with precision in the Santo Domingo text as synonymous with reconciliation (cf. 123). This leaves no room for a facile either-or. In fact reconciliation, like liberation, is an old and traditional Christian idea, which is nobody's private property.

18 This is a perspective adopted, not without difficulty, a long time ago in Latin America. It led to the description of the situation on the continent as a 'situation of sin' (Medellín, Peace 1). This viewpoint has clear biblical foundation. Hence it is also present in the universal magisterium of the church.

Translated by Dinah Livingstone

This essay was first published in *Páginas*, No. 119, January 1993.

Reflections on Collegiality
A Letter to My Brother Bishops

CÂNDIDO PADIN OSB

The calling of the Fourth Conference of Latin American Bishops in Santo Domingo offers us an opportunity to reflect on the criteria for the exercise of collegiality in the church, not only affectively, but also effectively. I would like to ask for your kind attention to the following reflections, which are entirely personal, completely unrelated to the function I exercise in the Brazilian Bishops' Conference. I am not motivated in this by the recent fact that my name was excluded (alone among all those elected by the Brazilian bishops) from participation in this conference. In any case, I am very pleased that my place will be occupied by my dear brother Dom Silvestre Luís Scandian, elected as first reserve. His dedication to pastoral planning and his concern to meet the needs of the deprived population of the outskirts of the cities (demonstrated on the occasion of the Pope's visit to Vitória), are ample credentials for his participation at Santo Domingo.

My main concern is to propose a change in the ways in which the agencies of the Holy See treat episcopates and, in particular, episcopal conferences. This is, of course, not the first time that we have been surprised by the way this relationship is conducted. The problem has been made worse, especially since the approval of the complementary legislation to the Code of Canon Law, drafted by episcopal conferences as provided in the Code itself.

None of us in his right mind would seek to challenge the undeniable gospel mandate of the primacy of Peter and his successors in the apostolic college and in the universal church. Indeed, Jesus described its exercise as a form of love (Jn 21:15-17). The issue is, rather, the way this primatial function is exercised, involving a genuinely human and fraternal attitude on the part of the successor of Peter towards his brothers in the faith, especially those whom the church has appointed as successors of the other apostles. It is to the person of Peter that Jesus entrusts the mission to 'confirm your brethren', a mission dependent on his conversion or (as others interpret) 'when you have returned to me' (Lk 22:32), denoting his identification with the preaching and life-style of the Master.

What happens, however, in fact, is that the relationship between the bishops and the Supreme Pontiff is rarely with him directly, but passes through innumerable collaborators in the Roman Curia, whose view of the church and personal attitudes are not always governed by the recommendations of the gospels. Decisions are sometimes even imposed in defiance of the rules of canon law, always with the claim that the action is taken in the Pope's name. Fortunately, our direct personal relationship with John Paul II has always been most cordial and attentive on his part, corresponding to the fraternal style recommended by Christ. It is a pity that it is not at these moments that the decisions and solutions are offered to the problems we bring to him. These go through the sieve of the usual criteria of the curial departments, and it is there that the regrettable distortions occur. There are, of course, honourable exceptions. Even during *ad limina* visits unpleasant scenes may occur, as I have witnessed myself, and bishops have told me of others.

Most clerics in the curia are still heavily influenced by the mentality and attitudes of European cultural colonialism, vestiges of an era in which there was a domination which ravaged the cultural values of the peoples of the Third World. The liberating message of the gospel, preached by the European missionaries who came to our lands, became enveloped in the cultural garb of the conquerors, who considered themselves bearers of civilisation to peoples whose culture was 'inferior' or even 'primitive'. There is a lamentable confusion between cultural level, which includes human and moral values, and technical progress, which is very often destructive of fundamental human values and encourages disrespect for rules of honesty. Very often communities belonging to peoples regarded by the First World as of inferior culture give examples of outstanding human wisdom and impressive fraternal solidarity. This applies to all cultures. Vatican II says that Christians should 'gladly and reverently lay bare the seeds of the word which lie hidden in them' (Vatican II, *Ad Gentes*, 11) The same conciliar decree (para 22) goes even further: 'Finally the young particular churches, adorned with their own traditions, will have their own place in the ecclesiastical communion, without prejudice to the primacy of Peter's See, which presides over the entire assembly of *charity*' [and not just of authority, I would add].

We have to recognise that this principle of respect for different cultural patterns, and for the resulting legitimate autonomy of the new particular churches, was not always observed by the Holy See, especially in the work of evangelisation in the nations of the Third World. The first years of the post-conciliar period found in the person of Pope Paul VI a very comprehensive and flexible attitude, consistent with his wise and courageous decision to continue and bring to a conclusion the Council providentially summoned by the prophetic figure of John XXIII. (The canonisation of both, awaited with anxiety, certainly deserves to be pushed forward faster than other processes.) In recent years, however, there have been increasing signs of a strong centralising tendency on the part of the agencies of the Holy See which is unnecessary and harmful to the gospel model of fraternity recommended by the primitive apostolic tradition and the recent Council.

Vatican II recognises that the variety of forms of development and organisation of ecclesial communities through the history of the church is a gift of providence. 'By divine Providence it has come about that various churches established in diverse places by the apostles and their successors have in the course of time coalesced into several groups, organically united, which, preserving the unity of faith and the unique divine constitution of the universal church, enjoy their own discipline, their own liturgical usage, and their own theological and spiritual heritage' (*Lumen Gentium*, 23). It sought to develop the rich vitality of the apostolic tradition, when it concluded: 'In like manner the episcopal bodies of today are in a position to render a manifold and fruitful assistance, so that this collegiate sense may be put into practical application' (ibid.). In other words, it can be seen that the Council wished to give the establishment of episcopal conferences the sense of rich vitality and originality of regional church forms in everything which does not affect 'the unity of the faith and the unique divine constitution of the universal church' (ibid.).

Following from this, the new Code of Canon Law ordered the establishment of episcopal conferences with the aim of 'promoting the greatest good which the church offers to human beings, principally in forms and varieties of apostolate duly adapted to the circumstances of time and place, in accordance with law' (Can. 447). Obeying this criterion of adaptation to regional and local circumstances, the Code specifies that conferences shall enjoy certain powers to promulgate complementary legislation to implement particular, explicitly indicated, instructions of the Code. This general attitude of the Code reflects one of the fundamental thrusts of the Council, namely to restore to the church the originality and vigour of the early period of Christianity by following the authentic tradition of the apostles. The apostles, as they passed through the most varied regions and nations, proclaiming the Good News, formed communities and appointed pastors to govern them and sustain and nourish community life, especially in the celebration of the Memorial of the Lord Jesus and in the preparation of new ministers of the Gospel. It was these pastors who ensured the permanent succession of the mission they received from Jesus: 'make disciples of all nations' (Mt 28:19). Appointed as successors of the apostles, bishops are

> the vicars and ambassadors of Christ. They govern the particular churches entrusted to them by their counsel, exhortations, and example, but also by their authority and sacred power... In virtue of this power, bishops have the sacred right and the duty before the Lord to make laws for their subjects, to pass judgment on them, and to make arrangements for everything pertaining to the ordering of worship and the apostolate... Nor are they to be regarded as vicars of the Roman Pontiff, for they exercise an authority which is proper to them, and are quite correctly called 'prelates', leaders of the people whom they govern (*Lumen Gentium* 27).

In view of these guidelines and principles, some attitudes and actions adopted by the Holy See towards our episcopal conference, the CNBB [National Conference of Brazilian Bishops, trans.] are very strange. Let us take just two examples. The Code of Canon Law provides, as a general rule, that a parish priest shall be appointed for an indefinite period. It adds, however: 'He may only be appointed by the diocesan bishop for a fixed period if this is allowed by decree by the episcopal conference' (Can. 522). In other words, the Code gave a specific power to conferences. It is the responsibility of the bishops in assembly to decide whether they wish to fix a specific minimum period for the appointment of parish priests. Now, when it came to draft the complementary legislation to the Code, our bishops, exercising their competence *de iure*, decided to set a minimum period of three years for these appointments. This decision was taken bearing in mind our situation, in that the shortage of clergy and frequent movement of our population requires frequent movements of parish priests. When the decision was communicated to the Holy See, the relevant curial body stated that it did not agree with the decision, and demanded that the bishops review it. At the following assembly, noting the Holy See's reply, the bishops considered the problem and decided by vote to maintain the previous decision and insist on its approval. On receiving a further rejection from Rome, our conference declared that it would await whatever decision the Holy See decided to take. The reply we received was the imposition of a minimum period of six years for such appointments. This was a clear violation of the provision of Canon 522, which specifies that setting a fixed period for the appointment of parish priests falls within the competence of episcopal conferences and not of the Roman Curia. Do the curial cardinals and monsignors who live in Rome know the situation of the church in Brazil better than our bishops? Is the arbitrary requirement of six years necessary to preserve 'the unity of faith and the unique divine constitution of the universal church' (*Lumen Gentium*, 23)?

Similar interference took place some years ago with the Holy See's insistence on the setting up of an episcopal doctrinal commission in the CNBB. We tried to explain on this occasion that this system of many isolated episcopal commissions for each sector, which we had previously tried in the CNBB, had revealed a number of disadvantages. Apart from making more difficult greater uniform coordination for general planning, it had the serious disadvantage of the high costs of air fares for the many members of the commissions in view of the great distances in Brazil. For this reason our experience made us decide in favour of a large commission of eight bishops (the CEP or Episcopal Pastoral Commission), elected by the episcopate, to coordinate the whole range of pastoral work, including all the sectors. Very often, however, the work of the CEP is supplemented by the collaboration of small groups of bishops with special competence in particular areas, and this occurs particularly during general meetings. I am not denying the valuable results achieved by the work of the Episcopal Doctrinal Commission, but these could also have been obtained by coordination between the CEP and a number of bishops with special qualifications in the issues raised by requests for expert doctrinal opinions. I note it, however, as a further imposition of the Holy See with regard to the conference's method of organisation, not laid down as of obligation by the Code. On the contrary, the Code provides for the establishment of commissions 'as the conference sees fit' (Can. 451). There is no respect for the ability of bishops to exercise their legitimate autonomy with regard to the way they organise their conferences, something which has nothing to do with the primatial function of the Pope. In practice, this amounts to considering us bishops immature and culturally inferior to the Roman prelates. Only they have the wise and correct criteria for directing the pastoral activities of the churches.

Finally, the same centralising and authoritarian attitude was shown in relation to the possibility of retired bishops being chosen to occupy posts of responsibility on conference bodies and being delegates to the Fourth Conference of the Latin American Bishops. At the 1991 assembly of the CNBB the Legal Commission was asked to interpret the rule in Canon 450#1 of the Code: 'Members of the conference are, *ipso iure*, all diocesan bishops of the territory and those equivalent to them in status, coadjutor bishops, auxiliary bishops and *the other titular bishops who exercise in the territory some special task entrusted to them by the Holy See or the bishops' conference....*' Considering this last section, which I have emphasised, the Legal Commission replied that there were three retired (titular) bishops at the assembly who fulfilled the necessary requirements and who could therefore be elected to posts open to election. On the basis of this interpretation the assembly elected me a member of the CEP. However, when the minutes were sent to the Holy See the Congregation of Bishops challenged my election, claiming 'that the *peculiare munus* (particular task) conferred by the Holy See or the bishops' conference was described in these terms in the process of preparation of the Decree *Christus Dominus*: "si peculiari aliquo munere fungerentur, cuiusmodi sunt v.g. Vicarius Castrensis, Rectores Universitatum Catholicarum, Adsistens Nationalis Actionis Catholicae (if they exercise some particular function such as military chaplain, rectors of Catholic universities, national assistant to Catholic Action)". In this text there is no mention of posts within the episcopal structure itself (president of an episcopal commission, etc.).' Unwilling to accept this challenge, the president of the CNBB asked the Prefect of the Congregation of Bishops to reconsider the case, sending him a carefully prepared opinion from the conference's legal experts in which, among other considerations, it noted that Canon 450#1 does not specify the *'peculiare munus'*, not restricting its interpretation to specific examples, merely requiring that it should be exercised in the territory of the conference. I would like to add a further consideration, which could throw light on other cases in the future. According to the best legal exegesis, the 'legislator's intention' cannot be identified with the motives of those who have prepared the text subsequently presented for a vote in the legislative body, in this case the bishops of the conciliar assembly. The bishops may have had a broader, not a restrictive, intention, which did not coincide with that of those who prepared the text. Once promulgated, the law must be interpreted *ut sonat*, 'as it reads', and no restrictions admitted except those expressly contained in it. Introducing restrictions is an illegitimate alteration of the text of the law.

When the case was brought to the Holy Father's attention by the Cardinal Prefect of the Congregation of Bishops, the Pope conceded 'on this occasion' the validation of my election as a member of the CEP. The legal consequence of this act of the Holy Father's was, unequivocally, that I am a member *ipso iure* of the conference, in the terms of Canon 450#1, at least during the current mandate of the CEP, since only a member of the conference can be elected. On this understanding the officers of the CNBB had no hesitation in including my name in the list of those who could be elected at this year's assembly as delegates to Santo Domingo, since the greater includes the lesser.

When I was elected on the second ballot, the officers sent the Congregation of Bishops the list of all the delegates elected for due confirmation. The reply, to their surprise was a curt message 'that it is not possible to accept the request that the retired bishop of Bauru, Dom Cândido Padin, should be a representative of the CNBB at the assembly of CELAM (?) in Santo Domingo,' without giving any reason for the refusal to confirm. With great zeal the president of the CNBB now sent a personal letter to the Holy Father requesting confirmation, *giaché non vediamo il perché della restritzione al suo nome*, 'since we do not see the reason for the objection to his name' (letter of Archbishop Luciano Mendes de Almeida). Nevertheless, the request, delivered personally by Dom Albano Cavallin, was not accepted, the Congregation of Bishops claiming that the list of names confirmed already issued by the Pontifical Commission for Latin America could not be altered.

The refusal to confirm this election is strange in view of the rule established by the Code for elections requiring confirmation: 'The competent authority, if it judges the person elected suitable in accordance with Can. 149#1, and if the election has been carried out in accordance with law, *cannot refuse confirmation*' (Can. 179#2). Now, as I showed above, the ratification of my election as a member of the CEP confirmed my status as a member *ipso iure* of the conference, which is sufficient suitability according to 'universal law' (Can. 149#1) to be elected as its delegate.

At the end of this account and the arguments which accompany it, I wish to make it very clear to my brother bishops that I am not demanding the approval of my election, which I regard as secondary. What does worry me is the lack of regard which is becoming customary for the exercise by bishops and their conferences of their legitimate autonomy and responsibility, especially in Latin America. The centralism of the Roman Curia, exercising authoritarian power, handing down decisions without adequate justification, is a very different model from the one recommended by the Council: 'It is through the loving exercise of authority by the apostles and their successors that Jesus Christ wishes his people to increase under the influence of the Holy Spirit' (*Unitatis Redintegratio*, 2). And the prince of the apostles himself urges us 'to tend the flock of God that is in your charge, exercising the oversight, not under compulsion but willingly, as God would have you do it – not for sordid gain but eagerly. Do not lord it over those in your charge, but be examples to the flock' (1 Pet 5:2-3).

I shall be very grateful to any of you who wish to let me know your opinion on these reflections.

With true collegial affection I greet all my brothers in prayerful communion with the sacrifice of Christ.

D. Cândido Padin OSB
Retired Bishop of Bauru
São Paulo, 15 August 1992

Contributors

Francis McDonagh has worked on church issues in Latin America for ten years at CIIR and was invited by a group of Latin American bishops to monitor the preparations for the Santo Domingo conference, which he covered as a journalist.

Jon Sobrino is a leading liberation theologian, and works in El Salvador. He was close to Archbishop Oscar Romero, who was murdered in 1980, and a member of the Jesuit community from which six members were murdered by the Salvadorean army in 1989. He was part of a back-up team of liberation theologians working from Mexico and supplying drafts to colleagues in Santo Domingo.

Gustavo Gutiérrez, a Peruvian priest, is known as 'the father of liberation theology' after his 1971 book, *The Theology of Liberation*, first systematised the ideas of the movement. Told by his bishop not to go to Santo Domingo, he was a member of the same theological team as Jon Sobrino during the Santo Domingo Conference.

Cândido Padin is a senior Brazilian bishop, now retired, who was one of the leaders of church opposition to the Brazilian military dictatorship of 1964-85. He is a member of the executive of the Brazilian bishops' conference and in charge of encouraging work with laity — a key theme at Santo Domingo. He was elected as a delegate to Santo Domingo by the Brazilian bishops, but then ruled ineligible by the Vatican. After the 1979 Puebla conference Bishop Padin produced a detailed list of the thousands of changes made by the Vatican to the document agreed by the bishops.